INDIVIDUAL AND COMMUNITY NATURE STEWARDSHIP

THE OLD PLACE

A NATURAL HISTORY OF
A COUNTRY GARDEN

INDIVIDUAL AND COMMUNITY NATURE STEWARDSHIP

THE OLD PLACE

A NATURAL HISTORY OF
A COUNTRY GARDEN

Merritt Gibson
With Illustrations by Twila Robar-DeCoste

LANCELOT PRESS
Hantsport, Nova Scotia

ISBN 0-88999-623-7
Published 1997

LANCELOT PRESS LIMITED, Hantsport, Nova Scotia.
Office and production facilities situated on Highway No. 1,
1/2 mile east of Hantsport.

MAILING ADDRESS:
P.O. Box 425, Hantsport, N.S. B0P 1P0

4

Dedication

To

Wilma, Elizabeth, Jamie and Glenys,
who share The Old Place with me.

CONTENTS

THE COUNTRY GARDEN

"Exploring nature is largely a matter of
becoming receptive to what lies all around you."

The Sense of Wonder
Rachel Carson, 1956

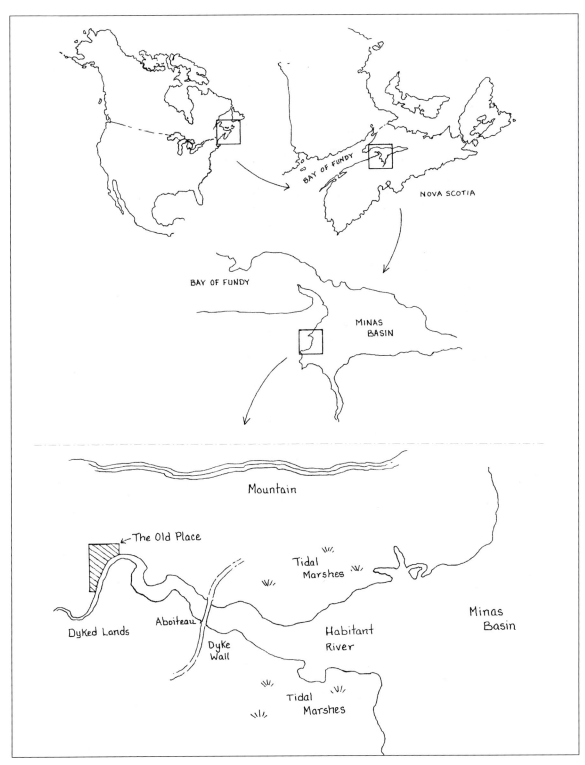

Mountain

The Old Place

Tidal Marshes

Dyked Lands

Aboiteau

Dyke Wall

Habitant River

Minas Basin

Tidal Marshes

BAY OF FUNDY

MINAS BASIN

NOVA SCOTIA

BAY OF FUNDY

THE OLD PLACE

We live at a time when many plant and animal populations are in decline and species are becoming extinct at an accelerating rate. Loss of habitat is the major cause. Globally, there appears to be little that most of us can do other than encourage and support those who are in a position to act. Locally, there is much that can be done for nature stewardship begins with individuals and communities. Individuals and communities can protect and restore natural sites, and help ensure the survival of the plants and animals that live in them. An appreciation of nature is prerequisite to such a goal.

The Old Place is in Canning, Nova Scotia, not very far from the Minas Basin where the twice-daily tides of fifteen metres and more are among the highest in the world; where the expansive tidal flats provide food for hundreds of thousands of migrating shorebirds; where the adjacent tidal marshes are home to a variety of plants and animals that are wonderfully adapted to live in such a harsh environment; and where the meadows, dyked years ago to stop flooding by the tide, are carpeted with wildflowers and patrolled by hawks and eagles.

Canning is a small village beside the Habitant River. It is surrounded by farmlands and tidal marshes, and backed by a forested mountain. Our house was built in the 1860s. Previous owners called it "The Old Place", and we kept that name. It sits on an upland, overlooking the lawns and gardens that slope down to the meadow and river.

I am a nature watcher with a special interest in birds. Our property of about eighteen acres includes lawns and cultivated gardens, a wooded area with overgrown thickets of wild roses, a small freshwater marsh and a meadow that borders the river. It is home through the seasons and years to many species of plants and animals, and the days are few that we do not walk or ski about the property to look for them.

More and more, here as elsewhere, people are watching and enjoying the wildlife about their homes. They appreciate the seasonal displays of wildflowers and look forward to the annual visits by migrating birds. There is much to see and there are many highlights on the local nature calendar.

Multiflora Rose

Nature Calendar

9

Dutchman's Breeches

The spring calendar begins in March when the geese arrive for a short visit before continuing their flight north. By late April, we hear the evening choruses of spring peepers and the winnowing sounds made by snipe as they circle and dive above the meadow. In May, the white flowers of shadbush and wild cherry decorate the countryside, warblers flit through the shrubbery, and vireos return as the leaves unfold. In late May, the apple and pear orchards start to blossom, bobolinks sing on the meadows as they begin their courtship displays, and spring-beauties and Dutchman's-breeches carpet the woodlands.

The fields are fragrant with wild roses in early summer, and later patches of daisies, hawkweed and vetch turn the meadows into mosaics of white, yellows and blues. Bird migration peaks again in September with visits by south-bound warblers and thrushes. Ducks collect on farm ponds in autumn, and maple and beech trees colour the mountain with reds and yellows. In winter, a few hundred eagles visit to feed on fish and other marine life stranded by the falling tide and on carrion put out for them by farmers. Sightings and numbers of eagles are daily topics of conversation.

Community Natural Places

While we enjoy discovering and watching the wild plants and animals that live all around us, they are continuously being lost to community and industrial expansion. Communities must include the conservation of natural places in their plans for development. The first step toward this goal is for each of us to become more knowledgeable about the natural world. The second step is to tell others so that they, too, may understand and enjoy nature. The third step is to work within our communities to conserve and restore natural sites and make them accessible to everyone. Natural places will be protected only when enough people appreciate and value the plants and animals that live in them.

THE GARDENS

One way to become more knowledgeable about the natural world is to have a special place, visit it regularly, and watch and listen carefully. Whether it is your backyard, a woodlot at the edge of town or a city park, you will soon become familiar with the plants and animals that live there and realize how dependent each species is on its particular habitat. You will then understand the importance of preserving that habitat and protecting the living things that are a part of it.

Cultivated Gardens

The lawns and flower gardens are behind the house and slope down to the meadow. They are enclosed by two driveways. The east driveway goes straight down the hill. The west driveway begins at the front entrance, encircles an old horse-chestnut tree, and then curves down and across the hill. The driveways meet at the stable, at the edge of the meadow.

A tall pine tree stands on the hill in one corner of the lawn, just outside the kitchen window. Woodpeckers, nuthatches, chickadees, warblers, thrushes and finches visit it through the seasons, and all take turns at the birdbaths and feeders on the ground below its branches. There is a hemlock tree on the opposite corner of the lawn. In winter, white-winged crossbills and evening grosbeaks sometimes decorate its branches.

Snowdrops and crocuses begin the spring season, followed by grape hyacinths, scillas, tulips and daffodils. Later come the poppies and lilies-of-the-valley. Flowering crab is the first tree to bloom each spring, then the apple and pear trees, and finally the English hawthorn.

There is an old honeysuckle bush near the back veranda. It blossoms in June and its flowers are favourites of hummingbirds. The flowers are ivory-coloured when they open in late afternoon, but change to a deep yellow overnight and remain open for a few days. The fruit ripens in August and attracts robins and other thrushes, catbirds, waxwings and rose-breasted grosbeaks. In late summer, migrating warblers feed on the insects about damaged fruit, and in winter downy woodpeckers and chickadees search over its branches for dormant insects and eggs.

Flower gardens border the curve of the driveway with beds

White-breasted Nuthatch

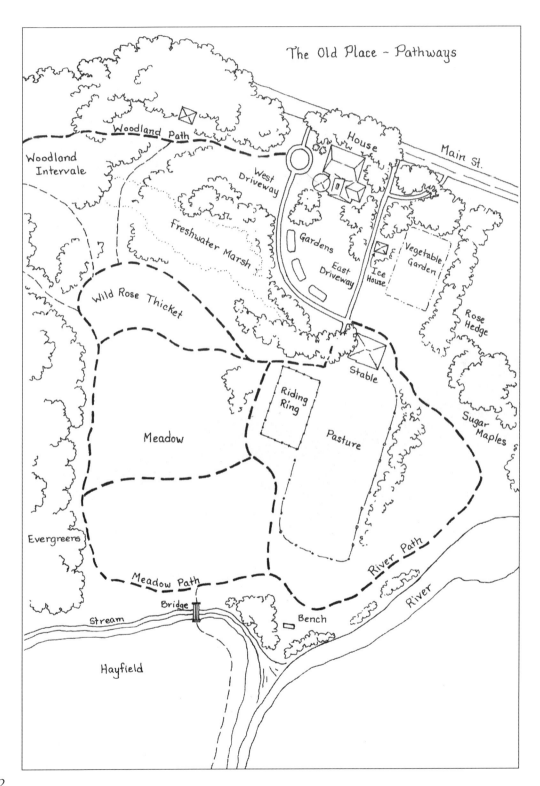

of Canterbury-bell, columbine, daisy, iris and lily. Plants such as mertensia, delphinium, bergamot, phlox and hollyhock provide a succession of flowers through the summer and early autumn. They produce a continuing supply of nectar and we spend many pleasant hours watching the hummingbirds, butterflies and moths that they attract.

Across the driveway, there is a wide border of spruce, willow and maple trees that continues into a wooded area. Ostrich ferns carpet the ground under these trees, and the deeper understory is a tangle of wild roses. Pheasants live there in winter, woodpeckers drum on dead and resonant branches in spring, and thrushes carol from these trees on summer evenings.

At the top of the driveway, about the front of the house, there is a bank of spiraea and several mockorange bushes. The spiraea bank is solid white when in flower each June. The mockoranges also blossom in June, and display large flowers with white petals arranged around a centrepiece of yellow stamens. Mockorange flowers remain open at night. They are especially bright in the moonlight and it is then that they release peak amounts of perfume. The garden must be visited at night to fully appreciate mockorange flowers, and to discover the many colourful moths attracted by their fragrance. Late evening is also the time to listen for crickets and watch for fireflies and bats.

Mockorange

An old ice house stands along the east driveway, half-way down the hill. Its walls and roof are three layers thick and the spaces between were once packed with sawdust for insulation. Late each winter it was filled with large blocks of ice cut on a neighbouring pond. In days before refrigerators, small chunks of ice were chipped off these blocks and carried into the house to a large, oak ice-chest in the pantry. Now day-lilies and irises grow along the north wall of the ice house and hollyhocks along its south wall. A red squirrel takes shelter in the roof during winter, and in spring a robin nests on a shelf under the eaves.

The vegetable garden is next to the ice house. We plant a large part of it in sunflowers and leave them there for the birds to help themselves. There is an old, twisted cherry tree beside the garden. Its dark, red fruit is delicious and enjoyed both by us and the robins.

Wild Gardens

We maintain a series of paths about the property for easier access to areas of interest. The main path follows the river and then circles the meadow, and there are side paths to good birding thickets and seasonal flower displays. Another path, the woodland path, begins at the front of the house and leads through a treed area before curving down to join the meadow path. We walk or ski these paths most days and watch a year-long pageant of plants growing, flowering and producing seeds; of leaves unfolding, enlarging, changing colours and falling; of summer birds arriving, nesting and congregating to leave; and of winter birds flitting through the branches, visiting feeders, or soaring high overhead to scan the countryside for food. Walking the same path, anticipating and watching the seasonal changes, is an ongoing source of pleasure and excitement.

River Path

The "walkabout" begins at the stable and passes down a bank covered with Jerusalem artichokes and touch-me-nots or jewelweeds. The artichoke is a type of sunflower but its flowers are small and not as showy as the cultivated ones. It produces large tubers that we sometimes dig up and slice into salads or boil like potatoes. They have a sweet taste and a crisp, watery texture. The touch-me-nots start to flower in late July and continue into September. We see three or four hummingbirds among these flowers during most walks in summer.

The path then passes along a grove of young sugar maples to the river. Broad-leafed cordgrass covers the lower half of the river bank and provides both shelter and food for wildlife. Pickerelweed and arrow-head form rafts of blue and white flowers on the water in July and August, and an abundance of nutlets in late summer that are quickly eaten by ducks. A family of muskrats lives on the river and we see one or two on most evening and early morning walks. With the break-up of ice in spring, common mergansers and goldeneyes dive for eels and invertebrates, and later great blue herons and sandpipers forage along the shore. Black ducks, teal and mallards are present during summer, and wigeons join them in autumn. The river freezes in winter and we can skate upstream or ski when snow covers the ice.

Jerusalem Artichoke

The walk continues along the meadow beside the river. Clumps of blue flags, butter-and-eggs, lupines and evening primroses grow along the path. Buckthorn bushes provide food and shelter for many birds, as do the bayberries that we planted for the yellow-rumped warblers. We also planted red-osier dogwood on the river bank and its tangles now provide shelter for pheasants, song sparrows and yellowthroats, as well as flat clusters of white flowers in June and reddish branches in winter.

There is a bench on a rise beside the river from which we can watch the wildlife in comfort. Sweet rockets, mostly white but some pink, carpet the river bank below the bench in spring, as do tansies, goldenrods and asters in late summer. It is relaxing to sit there in the evening and watch the swallows hawking for insects over the water and dipping for a drink. Sometimes at dusk, a barred or great horned owl glides by to begin a night of hunting on the meadow.

From the bench, the path turns away from the river and follows a hedge of multiflora rose across the meadow to a copse of evergreen trees. Here there are white pine, white and red spruces and balsam fir, together with a fronting of bayberry, cherry and buckthorn shrubs. Daisy, stitchwort, vetch, Queen Anne's lace, yarrow, and a variety of other plants provide a succession of colours throughout summer. Goldfinches and song sparrows eat the seeds in autumn as do tree sparrows and snow buntings in winter.

The path swings along the west border of the meadow and through a wooded intervale, where wild multiflora roses produce a flood of white blossoms in mid June. Many roses climb into the trees, that act like giant trellises, and form walk-through tunnels. In summer, the thickets are home to warblers, catbirds and waxwings. In fall and winter, the rose hips provide food for many birds, including about thirty pheasants.

Elm and white ash trees grow naturally in the intervale. We added spruce and fir for shelter and for kinglets, and red and sugar maples for warblers and vireos in spring and for red and yellow leaves in autumn. Two large elderberries produce white flowers in June, purple fruit for birds in August, and attractive buds on purplish stems in winter. A mockingbird spends the autumn and

Meadow Path

Butter-and-eggs

winter in the intervale, and one has done so for each of the past twenty-five years.

The path then returns to the stable, completing the circle of the meadow. It passes along a swampy area at the foot of the hill that is overgrown with wild roses, morning-glories, cattails and willows. The swamp is an ideal habitat for peepers and wood frogs in spring, and for flycatchers and warblers in summer.

Woodland Path

The woodland path begins at the front of the house and leads through a small area of red pine, oak, basswood and white birch. These are mature trees and form a closed canopy over the path. Young maple, spruce and cherry form the lower layer; and trillium and ostrich fern are present in the ground cover. This is where the red-eyed vireos nest, and where black-throated blue and other warblers forage during their pre-migratory wanderings in mid August.

Giant elms grow along the woodland path, and through the decades Virginia creeper has climbed to their top branches. In autumn, the yellow leaves of the elm and the scarlet leaves of the vines transform these trees into towers of colour.

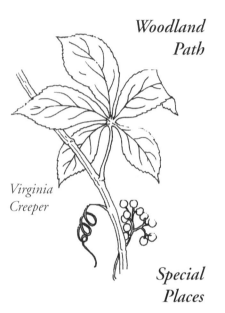

Virginia Creeper

Special Places

Having a special place and visiting it regularly is the best way to become acquainted with a natural community. You will soon look forward to the seasonal displays of wildflowers and visits by migrating birds. You will observe unique patterns of animal behaviour, curious associations between plants and animals, and a variety of adaptations that enables each species to live in its particular habitat. You will then appreciate the need to protect those habitats.

FLYING COLOURS

Attracting wildlife is another way to become more knowledgeable about the natural world. Whether by planting about our homes or caring for a community site, attracting wildlife creates special opportunities for observation and enhances our enjoyment of a garden or a wild area. In addition, we help maintain the habitats needed to keep wildlife about our homes and communities.

We plant flowers and shrubs to attract wildlife, and especially appreciate visits by hummingbirds and butterflies. Attracting wildlife permits close-up and ongoing observations of individual species and, with a few reference books to guide and explain our observations, greatly enhances our understanding of the natural world.

Hummingbirds

Three pairs of hummingbirds return to The Old Place each May. Presumably, they are often the same birds that nested here in previous years, for researchers believe that hummingbirds remember the locations of good food supplies. Larger numbers visit in August. August is the time when young birds are in flight and adult birds that nested elsewhere start wandering. Most importantly, the beds of nectar-rich hollyhock, phlox and touch-me-not start to flower in August. It is not unusual to see ten or twelve hummingbirds about these flower beds.

The ruby-throated hummingbird is the only species that nests at The Old Place. It is our smallest bird. It appears to be dark green with white underparts, and the male in proper lighting has a red throat. Actually, apart from the white areas, the feathers contain only black and brown pigments. However, microscopic pigment plates and air bubbles in the feathers refract light through a range of colours and make the feathers iridescent. The angle at which the light strikes the feathers alters the colours seen. The throat appears to be red when bright light is in front of the bird, but dark blue to nearly black when the light is from the side.

Hummingbirds make several sounds. The rapid beating of the wings causes the "humming" and is easily heard. However, we

Ruby-throated Hummingbird at Touch-me-not

Phlox

Hollyhock

must listen carefully to hear the high-pitched, twittering notes of their voices. Hummingbirds also make a roaring sound that may be especially loud when the male performs courtship flights. This sound results from air passing through the stiff outer tail and wing feathers and causing them to vibrate. The bird can alter this sound by spreading or closing these feathers.

Their flying ability is amazing and well worth the time taken to watch the performances. Hummingbirds fly forward, backward, hover and dart at speeds of up to 100 kilometres per hour; and their display flights include loops, "figures-of-eight" and other aerial acrobatics. These movements are possible because, unlike most birds, their wings generate power on the upstroke as well as the downstroke and, with changes in pitch, the wings act as rotors.

Sitting on the lawn and watching the hummingbirds about the flower beds and birdbath is one of the pleasures of a summer's afternoon. When feeding, they take short sips, and dart from flower to flower, or from port to port when at a feeder. They then perch on a twig, often on the nearby laburnum bush or pine tree, and rest for a few moments until their crops empty, after which they return to the flower beds for refills. Hummingbirds have long beaks and tongues, both needed to reach the nectar in deep flowers. Their tongues, coated with a sticky substance, also catch the insects and spiders that are inside the flowers.

While hummingbirds visit flowers of many types and colours, they prefer tubular-shaped flowers that hold large amounts of nectar and flowers that are red or orange. There are a number of plants at The Old Place that attract hummingbirds, and they produce a succession of blossoms from early spring through autumn. Horse-chestnut, weigela, Siberian pea, laburnum, honeysuckle, coral bell and mertensia flower in spring and early summer; delphinium, bergamot, garden balsam, geranium, phlox, morning-glory, nasturtium, hollyhock and impatiens flower in summer; and many of the summer plants continue to flower into autumn. Hummingbirds also require a good supply of water and are frequent visitors to birdbaths, and to plants laden with dew in early morning. They especially like moving water and we adjust the tap at the birdbath to give a fast drip.

Hummingbirds require a good food supply to maintain their high rate of activity. Researchers have calculated that every day hummingbirds must consume an amount of food that equals about twice their body weight. Hummingbird flowers produce nectars that contain high-energy sugars. Nectar also contains a small amount of protein. It is a dietary requirement, especially during the nesting period. Hummingbirds supplement the nectar protein by eating small insects and spiders.

One challenge each summer is to find a hummingbird's nest. Sometimes there is one saddled on the lower branches of a mountain ash tree beside the driveway. It is usually about two metres above ground and we watch it carefully until the young have flown. The nest is a delicate structure formed of lichens and mosses, bound together and to the branch by cobwebs and caterpillar silk, and lined with soft plant down. It is slightly larger than half a walnut shell and resembles a knot on the branch.

The female builds the nest and lays two white eggs during the latter half of June. The eggs are about the size of peas. The young hatch in two weeks and the female alone feeds them, making repeated trips to the garden for nectar and insects. The bills of the two young stick out above the nest like miniature antennae. The young leave the nest about two weeks after hatching. They forage about the flower beds and make frequent visits to the birdbath. Most hummingbirds leave in late August and September as the flowering season ends, although rarely we see one later in autumn.

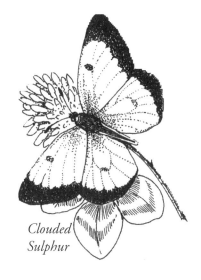

Clouded Sulphur

Butterflies

Butterflies also visit hummingbird flowers. They prefer open places with perches on which they can bask in the sunshine. Water is also important. A lawn or meadow with a small pond or birdbath, and flower beds that offer a succession of blossoms, are ideal sites for both butterflies and hummingbirds.

Butterflies visit all types of flowers, but prefer those with yellow, orange, red or blue blossoms. At The Old Place in spring, butterflies forage about the flowers of forget-me-not, sweet-William, verbena, honeysuckle, cherry, hawthorn, lilac, mockorange and spiraea. In summer, they visit day-lily, morning-glory, fuchsia and sweet alyssum. In late summer and early autumn, but-

Spring Azure

Painted Lady

White Admiral

terflies feed at zinnia, coneflower, cosmos, marigold, garden balsam, aster and phlox. Butterfly-bush, or buddleia, is a special favourite. All butterfly flowers are highly fragrant and rich in nectar.

Patches of wildflowers on the meadow also attract butterflies. They visit daisy, dandelion, vetch, hawkweed and red clover in early summer; yarrow, sow thistle, touch-me-not, boneset, Queen Anne's lace and white campion in late summer; and aster, goldenrod and blue thistle in early autumn.

While they visit many types of plants, butterflies show a preference for tubular flowers that store large quantities of nectar. They have long coiled tongues that uncoil to reach the nectar wells deep in these flowers. Butterflies also feed on the juice of fermenting fruit, and congregate in August about the honeysuckle bushes to feast on fruit damaged by birds.

Sometimes we see a number of butterflies congregated about a puddle on the meadow path, a practice known as "puddling". The males obtain sodium from the water and transfer it to the females during mating. The sodium is a requirement for egg development.

Many species of butterflies visit The Old Place each summer, although some occur more frequently than others. Clouded sulphurs are often abundant on the meadow and dance about patches of clover and other legumes. So also are the beautiful spring azures, especially about beds of lupins in spring and tangles of vetch in summer. Painted ladies are more numerous in some years than in others. They often travel in groups and, in late summer, a dozen painted ladies clustered on a blue thistle is a delightful sight. The strikingly marked white admirals are most numerous in July.

Mourning cloak is one of the first to appear each spring. It may appear on warm days in early April, but we see it most often during the latter half of May and early June. It is a large butterfly, dark brown or almost black, and its wings are beautifully marked with blue spots and a yellow border. Mourning cloak appears early because it overwinters in the adult form. The adults winter in sheltered places, such as behind loose bark, and emerge in spring when the temperatures reach about 16° C. On cool days, we sometimes see a mourning cloak basking in the sun with wings outstretched to absorb the warmth.

The mourning cloak lays its eggs in spring on the leaves of birch, willow and elm trees, and then dies. The eggs hatch in early summer, and adult mourning cloaks are again about the gardens in early July. However, the mourning cloaks seen in summer are from the first brood of the year and are not the individuals that overwintered.

Mourning cloaks become dormant during the dry period of mid summer and sightings of them are infrequent. They start to emerge in mid August and are commonly seen again in late August and September, often feeding on sap about tree injuries and on the juice of damaged fruit. In late September and October they find a sheltered place in which to hibernate for the winter. Mourning cloaks live for almost a year, longer than most butterfly species.

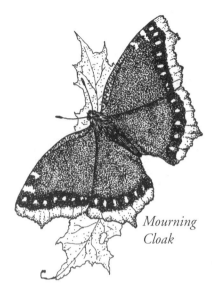

Mourning Cloak

Tiger swallowtails are also frequent visitors and black swallowtails visit from time to time. Tiger swallowtails are strikingly coloured: bright yellow with black markings, thus the name "tiger". On warm sunny days in June and July, we might see a dozen or more of them during a walk about the garden and meadow. Swallowtails are so-named because each hind wing projects to form a "tail". Swallowtails flutter and sail from flower to flower in what appears to be an effortless fashion, but they are also vigorous flyers and can quickly cross the meadow and lawns.

Tiger Swallowtail

The American copper is another common butterfly about the gardens and fields. It is a smaller butterfly, orange or coppery and with gray markings. The wings may be quite iridescent, usually reflecting light in the red to orange range. Coppers are present from spring to mid autumn. They are most plentiful in July and August when sheep sorrel, curled dock and blunt-leaved dock, their favourite plants, are in flower. Coppers are fun to watch. They usually perch quietly on a plant and bask in the sun; but they are fast flyers and readily challenge other butterflies that enter their territories.

American Copper

The American copper is not a native butterfly. The early settlers introduced it from Europe. Interestingly, the docks and sheep sorrel are also European plants. The French settlers brought sheep sorrel here some 300 years ago.

Colour and Activity

Planting for wildlife enhances our appreciation for living things. Special plantings attract a variety of species to our homes and communities. Many species are brightly coloured, others show interesting behaviours, and all are fun to watch. Attracting wildlife adds both colour and activity to gardens and community sites.

THE GARDEN AT NIGHT

Wild and cultivated flowers and shrubs attract hummingbirds, butterflies, moths and other wildlife. They visit during both night and day. However, the habitats required to support these species are continuously being lost, and many of these plant and animal populations are in decline. Gardeners can help by planting flowers and shrubs that attract these animals. Communities can also help by sowing wildflowers in unused lots and along highways. All add colour, awareness, and a variety of species to discover and watch.

While there are many plants and animals to look for in the garden during the day, there are other species to discover at night. Many people fail to explore the world that exists after dark, but its exploration greatly enhances our knowledge of the natural world that lives all around us. The variety of night life is large, and the adaptations to life in the dark are many and fascinating.

On spring nights there are choruses of peepers mixed with the hoarse notes of wood frogs, and sounds of migrating geese talking to one another as they fly overhead. A summer's night begins with thrushes carolling and nighthawks calling and then "booming" as they pull out of their dives. Later, crickets chirp and trill, fireflies flash in the dark, and bats flutter about the lawn. Migrating birds fly across the face of the moon in autumn, and moths fly about trees and lights on warm winter nights.

Several flowers open and are highly scented at night, and the garden must be visited at that time to enjoy them. The white flowers of the old-fashioned tobacco plant, *Nicotiana*, open in the late evening, as do wildflowers like white campion and evening primrose. Many garden flowers, including lily, Canterbury-bell, foxglove and alyssum, are open during both day and night, but produce perfume in peak amounts at night. The accumulation of perfume often makes these flowers moist and sticky. Pink, yellow and white flowers are especially vivid on clear nights. These are the ones that attract moths.

Many night-flowering plants depend on moths for pollination. The plants attract moths by producing large quantities of

Flowers and Moths

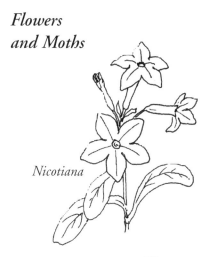

Nicotiana

23

Luna Moth

Cecropia Moth

Hummingbird Moth

nectar, more so than many day-flowering plants, and the moths feast on it. The perfume, a by-product of nectar production, also lures pollinators to the flowers. A few night flowers, like evening primrose, reflect light of the ultraviolet type. While we cannot see ultraviolet light, some moths can and the light guides them to the nectar wells. Many daytime flowers also use ultraviolet light to guide pollinators.

Several types of moths can be discovered by exploring flower beds and shrubs at night. Using a flashlight may help, but allowing your eyes time to adjust and exploring by moonlight gives a better appreciation of the night garden. Also, having a place in your garden designed for night viewing, with special plantings of both cultivated and wild species and away from light pollution, should assure many exciting discoveries.

Finding a luna moth is always exciting. It is most numerous in early summer, and is one of our largest and most beautiful moths. Its wings are pale green and extend into curved tails, and both fore and hind wings have large spots. These "eye-spots", as those of many moths, are believed to distract or frighten predators.

The cecropia moth is plentiful in early summer, and is also an exciting discovery. Cecropia has a wing-span of up to fifteen centimetres. Its wings are brown, shaded with red, and both fore and hind wings have crescent-shaped "eye-spots". Its body is also reddish with darker bands and a white collar.

Several kinds of sphinx moths, or hawk moths, visit flowers at night to sip nectar, and are also attracted to artificial lights. They are large moths and visit most often in June and July. Sphinx moths hover above the flowers and their wings produce a "humming" sound. In flight, they are easily mistaken for hummingbirds for their wingbeats are fast and blurred. One of the smaller sphinx moths is called the "hummingbird moth". Its colours resemble those of a hummingbird: a greenish body tinged with red and reddish-brown wings. Hummingbird moths are active during both day and night.

Night-time Singing

Listening is as important as seeing when exploring the garden at night. The sounds of crickets provide a concert each evening in late summer and early autumn. Crickets are numerous about the gardens and meadows, where the thick growth provides both humidity and shelter. Cricket sounds or "songs" consist of a series of chirps and trills, and only the males produce them in most species. A stridulating organ located on the fore wings makes both sounds. It is made up of two parts: a file-like series of ridges on one wing and a scraper on the other wing. The "songs" are produced by rubbing the wings together, and are "heard" by a special organ located on the cricket's fore legs. The frequency and pitch of the trills is related to temperature. They become less numerous, slower and of lower pitch as the temperatures cool in late summer and fall.

Field and tree crickets are present at The Old Place. We look for field crickets in the uncut grass of borders and on the meadow. They are black and easy to find. Field crickets chirp to guard their territories and sound alarms, and trill during courtship while they dance about the females. The tree crickets are more difficult to locate, but we find them climbing about the branches of shrubs. They are slender and dark green with pale-green wings. The tree crickets also chirp and trill, but their sounds are higher in pitch than those of field crickets. Male and female crickets are easily distinguished: the male has a rounded abdomen, the female has a spike-like ovipositor at the end of her abdomen through which she deposits eggs into soil or rotting wood.

The light-flashing of fireflies or "lightning bugs" is a familiar sight on summer evenings. Most years, fireflies are plentiful about the lawns and meadows at The Old Place. The uncut meadow, where they can hide under the vegetation during the day, is excellent firefly habitat. The luminous or light organ is at the tip of the abdomen. It releases an enzyme that drives a reaction which burns atmospheric oxygen to produce the flash. The light is especially bright because highly reflective crystals or uric acid surround the light organ. Light-flashing is part of the mating ceremony. The various kinds of fireflies have different flash patterns, and experts can identify the species and sometimes the sex by watching the flashes.

Both sexes flash, but only the males fly and the signals seen

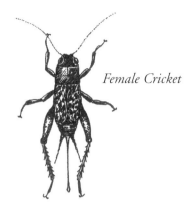

Female Cricket

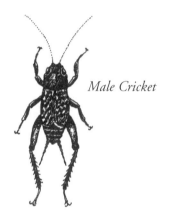

Male Cricket

Lights in the Dark

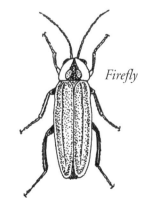

Firefly

25

are usually those of the males. The female flashes from a perch or the grass to attract the male, and he flashes in reply. The female mates only with a male displaying the flash pattern typical of her species. The larvae also flash. They live in the grass and flash to attract the small insects and other organisms on which they feed.

Winter Moths and Moths in Winter

Summer is not the only season to look for night-time insects. Some insects are active in late autumn and winter. Studying these animals reveals several behaviours and adaptations that enable them to remain active and reproduce under conditions of cold temperatures.

One species is called the winter moth. It is most numerous in late autumn and early winter, when the temperatures are within a few degrees of 0° C. After sunset the males start fluttering about our windows, attracted by the light, and continue to do so during much of the night. They are also about on cloudy days.

Winter Moth

Male winter moths are beige with darker brown mottling, a pattern of camouflage that blends with the tree bark on which they rest, and they have large, wide wings. Researchers have shown that the metabolic rate of these moths is low and their wing-beat is slow, much slower than that of summer moths. However, their broad wings enable them to remain airborne, and the slow wing-beat conserves energy at a time of limited supply. In such ways, these moths are able to fly and find mates at low temperatures.

The females are more difficult to find. They live in the litter at the base of trees. They lack wings and look like larvae with long legs. On warm winter evenings they crawl up the trunks and release "pheromones" or sex hormones to attract males. The eggs are laid in crevices in the bark and within patches of lichens on the trees, and the young hatch in early spring. The caterpillars feed on tree leaves and may do considerable damage. However, in winter, chickadees, brown creepers, nuthatches and woodpeckers eat the eggs and help control caterpillar numbers.

Eupsilia Moth

Eupsilia is another moth that sometimes is active on winter nights. It belongs to a family of moths that are often called owlet moths because their eyes are bright and their bodies are "furry". Researchers have shown that the life-style of *Eupsilia* is different from that of the winter moth. *Eupsilia* lives for much of the winter in piles of dead leaves and other debris where, covered with snow, the temperatures remain within a few degrees of freezing. However, the adults appear during warm periods and are particularly noticeable about windows during the "February thaw".

Unlike the winter moths, the wing-beat of moths like *Eupsilia* is fast and comparable to that of summer moths. These "cold-blooded" animals undergo a period of shivering, a pre-flight "warm-up", to generate the heat needed by the muscles to sustain flight. This heat is concentrated in the thorax by the circulatory system, which is designed as a heat exchange system. That is, the vessels conducting the warmed blood away from the thorax are adjacent to those conducting cooler blood into the thorax, and the heat is transferred to the incoming blood. In addition, a thick "furry" covering insulates the thorax and limits heat loss. In these ways, the temperature within the thorax is maintained above 32° C, as in summer moths. This enables the wing muscles to work and permits these moths to fly, although the air temperatures are within a few degrees of 0° C.

Many insects fly at night in summer and so do the bats that feed on them. Bats are superb insect catchers, and are numerous over the lawns and meadows at The Old Place. The best part about watching bats is that it can be done from the comfort of a lawn chair or a hammock. Most bats fly within a few metres of the ground, and watching from a low hammock gives a better appreciation of bat numbers than standing and looking upwards.

The saying "blind as a bat" is misleading. Bats have excellent sight. In addition, bats have an echolocation or sonar system. They emit a variety of supersonic clicks and twitters, that are inaudible to our ears, and are guided by the echoes bouncing off buildings, trees, insects and other solid objects. Researchers believe that bats use vision to see objects at a distance and echolocation to recognize objects that are close.

Bats hunt at night and feed on insects that they locate with the help of their echolocation system. Their apparent "haphazard" flight pattern is often a search pattern or a path from insect to insect. One bat may catch an estimated 3000 insects per night. However, a few insects, like lacewings, can hear bat calls and

Superb Insect Catchers

Little Brown Bat

Lacewings

manoeuvre to escape. Some moths also hear bats and dive to evade them, and a few moths emit sounds to confuse the bats.

Bats sleep during the day, usually in a dark place in a building, or under eaves or a flake of loose bark. There, we see them hanging head downward, perhaps so they can launch quickly into flight. A single young is born in June. The mother carries the baby with her for the first few days, and then leaves it in a communal nursery until it is able to fly. Young bats follow their mothers in flight by listening to their echolocation signals.

The little brown bat is the most numerous species about The Old Place. The Eastern long-eared bat, or Keen's bat, occurs regularly and the Eastern pipistrelle is an occasional visitor. In October, these three bats seek the shelter of caves where they over-winter. Bat caves must be deep enough to maintain a high humidity and an above-freezing temperature through the winter. There are no bat caves about The Old Place, but there are some in a river bank about eighty kilometres away. Up to 8000 bats winter in one of these caves. Cave bats become dormant in winter. That is, their metabolism decreases, they live on stored fat and do not feed, and their body temperature drops to that of their surroundings. They do awake and flutter about the cave from time to time and drink water. Banding returns show that the little brown bat may live for up to thirty-five years.

Some evenings we see a large, "falcon-like" silhouette flying about the tree tops. It is presumably a "tree bat" for they live and forage in tall trees. The one at The Old Place is likely the hoary bat, but we have not identified it with certainty. The hoary bat is our largest bat, with a wing-span of forty centimetres. It is reddish-brown with a silvery "frosting", thus its name. The red bat and silvered-haired bat are also local tree bats, but we have not yet identified either at The Old Place. Tree bats, unlike cave bats, migrate south for the winter season, perhaps as far as the Carribean, and return in May. During migration, they sometimes land on fishing boats sixty kilometres and more off the coast of Nova Scotia.

A World Worth Exploring

The world at night is different from the one seen during the day. Plants and animals adapt in many ways to meet the special conditions of darkness: high nectar production, ultraviolet and perfume guides, enhanced vision, light and sound systems, echolocation mechanisms and temperature controls. Night-time presents a new and curious world, one worth exploring.

SONGBIRDS IN THE GARDEN

With a special knowledge of one area, naturalists can gather much useful information on nesting success and variations in bird populations. Increasingly, this information now records declines in the local populations of certain species. Initially, such declines are often not even recognized. Such documentation, however, gives an early emphasis to the need for individuals and communities to protect and restore nesting habitats and food sources.

A number of songbirds summer at The Old Place and we spend many pleasant hours watching and listening to them. We planted flowers and shrubs about the house to attract birds, and these plus the dense thickets and tall trees in the background form attractive habitats. Some songbirds are plentiful but eight or ten species, although frequently seen a decade ago, are now less common.

American Robins

The songbird season begins each spring with the arrival of robins. From mid February onward, as we eagerly await spring, it is reassuring to know that the robins are on their way. Many of our robins winter in Florida and neighbouring states and, beginning in February, flock after flock start their journey north. Their migration is a leisurely one, with frequent stops to rest and eat. Robins do not migrate to the "cold" north, but follow the spring thaw. They proceed north as the weather warms and fly within a temperature zone where the day-night average is about 2° C. They arrive in southern New England about March 10, in Maine about March 19 and, provided there are no storms in the Gulf of Maine, at The Old Place within a day or two of March 24.

The first flock we see foraging on the lawn is usually one of thirty to forty birds. However, one March we counted a record number of 176 robins in the backyard. Most visit only briefly and then continue their journey; but a few are "home", for the same individuals often return to the garden where they nested the previous year. While counts are high at migration times, weekly counts taken throughout the summer usually record twelve to fifteen robins on most walks.

Robin

Robins start singing within a few days of arrival. It is usually the male robin that sings, often perched on a low branch with his head held high. Robins sing most frequently in spring and early summer, but also from time to time throughout summer and early autumn. They have a variety of songs and calls that reflect both different situations and different moods. The morning and evening songs are our favourites and carols during spring showers are always cheerful. Their songs consist of two- or three-note phrases, repeated over and over with variations. During the breeding season, robins begin singing well before sunrise and are often the first singers heard each morning. They apparently prefer dim light for they sing not only in the early morning and again in the late evening, but also on cloudy days and during nights when the full moon lights the countryside. We listened to robins singing during the eclipse of the sun that occurred on July 10, 1972, on an otherwise sunny day; and a naturalist friend, Sherman Williams, noted the same phenomenon during the solar eclipse on May 10, 1994. Both observations nicely illustrate the robins' preference for singing in dim light. On these occasions, the time of darkness was noticeably quiet but, curiously, robins burst into song during the dim light before and after the period of dark, just as they do in the evening and early morning.

Robin's nest

Several pairs of robins nest at The Old Place. It is difficult to know how many because one pair often raises two or more broods and builds a new nest for each. We make a nest survey in early winter after the leaves have fallen. The nests, constructed of coarse grass about a cup of mud, are easy to recognize. We found eight nests on one survey: two along the woodland path, five within the rose thickets and hedges on the meadow, and one in the hawthorn tree on the lawn.

Robins begin building their nests in late April. It is then that we see them carrying clumps of mud and grass in their beaks. They often build their first nest in the spruce and pine trees along the meadow path, for conifers offer better concealment and shelter in early spring before the deciduous trees are in leaf. However, they construct later nests also in deciduous trees and shrubs, and a pair nests each year in a tree on the lawn. Robins prefer to nest near open, grassy areas where they can easily drop down to search for food on the ground. Gardens and lawns with trees and shrubs are ideal sites.

Young "speckled" Robin

Robins start laying eggs, usually four, in May. The eggs hatch in about two weeks. The female alone incubates the eggs and leaves the nest only for brief periods to feed. After hatching, the young remain in the nest for two more weeks and both parents bring food to them. The first brood fledges in late June, and the speckled young scamper about the lawn practising the techniques of catching insects and other invertebrates. Once the young have fledged, the female leaves to lay another set of eggs in a second nest and the male remains to feed the first brood. The young robins of the second nesting are present about the lawn in August.

Robins search over the lawn for food, looking for worms, snails, spiders, caterpillars, beetles and other insects. They forage at all times of the day, but prefer the early morning while the ground is still moist with dew. Another favoured time is during a gentle spring rain. Robins hunt by carefully searching one spot, and then running across the lawn to explore another spot. They are not listening for worms when they tilt their heads, but are watching intently for the slightest movement that might mean a juicy morsel. Robins add fruit to their diet in late summer and autumn, including those of honeysuckles, blueberries, blackberries and, later, mountain ashes and roses. While they consume some fruit of commercial value, they also consume enormous numbers of insects that damage these crops.

In September and October, the robins start gathering in rose thickets on the meadow. These thickets offer protection and a plentiful supply of food. At such times, it is possible to find up to 200 robins about the property. Late one October a flock of 196 robins flew from a rose thicket while we were birding on the meadow. Usually when disturbed, robins circle and alight in a nearby thicket. On this occasion, they circled high into the sky and flew away toward the mountain. Presumably, they were starting the next lap of their migration during which they follow the mountain range to the south and west. Within a few days another flock of 100 robins gathered in the rose thickets, and a third flock of 70 robins visited the following week. These birds stop to replenish the energy supplies needed for the next lap of their flight south. Successful migration requires clean feeding areas along the routes, and protecting or providing them is an important part of bird stewardship.

We first see barn swallows circling over the meadow in early May. They prefer open spaces where they can wheel widely and hawk for insects. They also like to swoop along water where they can dip for a drink or a quick splash-bath without interrupting their flight. The meadow and river provide their preferred habitats.

Like robins, barn swallows return to the same nesting site each year. At The Old Place, they nest in the horse stable, usually one or two pairs, and one of our first jobs each spring is to open the doors to the hay loft for them. We especially appreciate the barn swallows for legend claims that they symbolize hope and good luck.

The barn swallows begin their courtship flights shortly after arrival, with each pair sailing gracefully over the meadow and along the river. The male trills and twitters continuously during these flights. Barn swallows build a nest of mud pellets stuck together with saliva, and with pieces of hay between the pellets for binding. They line the nest with grass and feathers. The swallows collect the mud from puddles on the meadow. Construction is slow, allowing time for an area of pellets to dry before adding to it, and may take more than a week. Barn swallows build a new nest each year, but often by adding to the top of an old one. There are stacks of nests ranging from three to eight tiers high in the hay loft.

The barn swallows lay four or five eggs in June. The young hatch in about two weeks, but remain in the nest for an additional three weeks before flying. The young swallows often return to the nest to rest. Both parents bring food to the nestlings and for a few days to the fledglings. Barn swallows lay a second set of eggs in mid July, either in the same nest or in another one newly built nearby. The young of the first nesting help feed the second brood. However, in years when temperatures remain cool, the barn swallows nest later than usual and raise only one brood. We enjoy

Barn Swallows

Barn Swallow

hearing their constant twittering while we are working about the stable. Often in the evening, the entire swallow family lines up along the wires to watch us and seem to enjoy human company.

We see eight to twelve barn swallows on most walks throughout summer, although not all nest at The Old Place. During the second half of August, as migration time approaches, they start to congregate over the meadows and along the river. On some evenings, we count over a hundred swallows. They leave in early September, although an occasional straggler may appear briefly during October and early November.

Yellow Warblers

Yellow warblers spend the summer in the garden, attracted by the many shrubs and trees. They frequent the lilac, spiraea, mockorange and honeysuckle bushes. They also inhabit the thickets of multiflora rose on the meadow. We see six to ten yellow warblers on most walks between May and the end of August.

The yellow warblers return in mid May. We usually hear the male singing first and then, with a little searching, we find the singer perched on the uppermost branch of a shrub or on top of a small tree. There, with head held upward, he pours forth his songs. The song is loud and distinctive, a series of high-pitched notes, sometimes described as "tsee, tsee, tsee, tsee, wee". He sings repeatedly during the courtship and nesting periods, often singing several songs per minute.

Yellow Warbler

Yellow warblers build their nests in late May and early June. We find one or two nests most years, usually in a thick spiraea or rose thicket and tightly bound around several small branches. Yellow warblers construct their nests of fine grass and plant fluff, and often include horse hair that they collect from the fence around the pasture. They lay four or five eggs in early June. The young hatch in about twelve days and remain in the nest for an additional two weeks before flying. Both parents feed the young, sometimes as frequently as once every few minutes.

Yellow warblers busily flit through the shrubs and trees searching for insects, and pause only to sing and feed their young. They capture all types of insects, including many garden pests. Thus, in addition to bright colours and cheerful songs, their feeding preferences make them valued visitors to the garden.

The property counts for robins, barn swallows, yellow warblers and several other garden birds have not changed in recent years. However, the numbers for some garden songbirds, including the rose-breasted grosbeak and gray catbird, have declined. Furthermore, researchers predict that other common species may also become scarce during the next one or two decades. It is difficult to imagine a garden without them.

The rose-breasted grosbeaks arrive at The Old Place in early May. The male is strikingly coloured: black and white with a scarlet breast. The female is brown and white, streaked, and with orange underwings that show in flight. Grosbeaks are colourful additions to the spring garden. However, their spring visit is a short one and they soon leave to nest in the open deciduous woods on the mountain.

We know of a wooded area on the mountain where they nest, and plan a trip there each spring just to hear them sing. The male grosbeak sings, often perched in full view on a branch partway up a maple tree where the shadows of fluttering leaves dapple his bright colours. His loud notes are clear and melodious and not unlike the carolling of a robin.

Rose-breasted grosbeaks return to The Old Place in August. They stay for a longer visit on this occasion and feed on the abundance of fruit in the thickets. Until a few years ago, we could find three or four grosbeaks on most walks during August; and their numbers increased to twenty-five or more during the first week in September with the arrival of the migrants. These numbers dropped to ten or twelve birds in the second week of September, and most had left by the third week. However, the number visiting The Old Place has declined during the past few years. We can still find them nesting on the mountain, but now only three or four birds visit the property in late summer.

The catbird first appears in late May and is a delightful visitor to the garden. Catbirds prefer gardens with overgrown shrubbery. They are secretive birds and skulk in the bushes, although one may perch briefly, flicking its tail, on a branch arching above a thicket. When we are sitting on the lawn, one often

Property Counts

Rose-breasted Grosbeaks

Rose-breasted Grosbeak

Gray Catbird

35

Gray Catbird

hops through the nearby shrubbery and cautiously peers out to watch us. The scientific name for the catbird is an appropriate one, for *Dumetella* means "thicket".

Catbirds produce a variety of songs and sounds, other than the frequently heard "mewing" calls, and some are quite melodious. They mimic other birds and animals and may even imitate inanimate sounds. Catbirds call repeatedly from the middle of a thicket, or from a favourite perch, and sing during both day and night.

Catbirds are most in evidence during courtship, when the male chases the female from one thicket to another and about the lawn. Their nest is a large mass of twigs, hidden in dense shrubbery. The female lays four beautiful, bluish-green eggs in June. The young hatch in about two weeks and remain in the nest for an additional two weeks before flying. Later, catbirds construct a second nest and raise another brood. Usually the first young remain nearby and help feed the second brood. The catbirds leave in September.

Until a few years ago, we regularly saw two or three catbirds during a walk about the property and at least two pairs nested here. Now we see catbirds only occasionally and doubt that they still nest at The Old Place.

Population Declines

Is the decline of such species as rose-breasted grosbeaks and catbirds a local phenomenon? Is it widespread? Is it a short-term one? Will the numbers soon be restored? Is it a permanent loss? Bird numbers may vary from year to year for several reasons: birds may move out early following a cold spring; nesting failure one year results in reduced numbers the next year; and birds travel widely in search of new sources of food. Declines for these and other such reasons are often of a short-term duration.

Population declines caused by loss of habitat are different. Whether the loss is in summer nesting territories, along the migration routes or in wintering sites, it leads to a long-term and likely a permanent change. Short-term versus permanent declines are difficult to distinguish in their initial stages, for we simply do not have sufficient information for many species. However, each year a Breeding Bird Survey is now conducted across North America by volunteer birders. This work is establishing an essential database that will help assess long-term population changes at the local, regional and continent-wide levels.

Early recognition of population declines is crucial if food sources and nesting habitats are to be improved and protected while some birds are still present. Local observers are best able to compile the documentation needed and initiate the appropriate actions. Monitoring and stewardship programmes are urgently needed if we are to keep some species about our homes and communities, and continue to enjoy their songs and bright colours.

Community Observers

STEWARDSHIP

There is much that individuals and communities can do to help wildlife. Projects to protect wildlife also encourage awareness, record useful information about local species, and build a database to help define and support future recommendations and actions. Naturalists must accept a role in community leadership if we are to conserve wild plants and animals and enhance the quality of human life associated with the enjoyment of nature.

The number of people interested in nature increases each year. They enjoy the outdoors, appreciate plants and animals, and want to take part in natural history and conservation projects. Here, as elsewhere, individuals and communities are organizing such projects and many are remarkably successful.

Short-eared Owls

Occasionally we flush a short-eared owl during a walk across the meadow in early morning, or see one fluttering about like a large moth at dusk. The short-eared owl is not a common nesting bird in Nova Scotia. Nevertheless, its numbers have declined in recent years.

These owls nest locally on dykelands, often in well-established hayfields. However, with new hay varieties that mature earlier and the need to harvest two crops each summer, haying now begins in late June and birds that have not fledged by that time may be inadvertently killed by the mowers. A few summers ago a mower passed through a nest and killed the mother, who remained on the nest, but it passed over the young protected under the mother and they survived. A naturalist transferred the owlets to another nest with young. The foster owls cared for them and they later fledged.

Recognizing the problem, George Alliston, a concerned naturalist, enlisted the assistance of the local Blomidon Naturalists Society and launched an on-going study to monitor nesting and try to improve nesting success. George prepared a pamphlet about this threatened species and a statement of his proposal, and presented them to the farmers who owned the hayfields. All farmers

Short-eared Owl

fully supported the proposal, for they recognized the value of these birds in controlling rodents. Twenty-eight volunteers from the naturalists society joined the project.

Each year, twice weekly from April through early June, the volunteers undertake a systematic survey of over 9000 acres of dykelands for short-eared owls. They work from the roadways so as not to trespass on farmers' fields. Fields where nesting is suspected are then visited, with the farmers' permission, by two birders experienced in locating nests. When they locate a nest, one observer approaches and attempts to estimate the stage of nesting or the ages of the chicks. They inform the landowner and, if it is decided that nesting will continue into the haying season, they flag the site and the farmer mows around it.

It will require several years to determine the true status of the short-eared owl and the success of this programme. Nevertheless, the programme illustrates a common pattern: a naturalist recognized a problem and prepared a plan of action, the property owners once informed co-operated fully, and interested volunteers joined the project. In time, our hope is that the local short-eared owl population will be restored. In the meantime, many people now are aware of this species and have a better understanding of dykeland habitats.

Sometimes when we are sitting by the river at dusk, a barred owl glides past to begin a night of hunting on the meadow. They hunt over the fields for small mammals and along the edge of the river for amphibians. Barred owls also fish. It is fun to watch an owl perch on a log over the water, wait and watch, and suddenly drop to snatch a fish that swam too close to the surface. Their fishing techniques are remarkably successful. It is also exciting to visit the woodlands at dusk in early spring, to imitate the owl's eight- or nine-note call, "Who-cooks-for-you? Who-cooks-for-you-all?", and wait for a reply. The challenge then is to call the owl through the trees to a nearby branch.

Although once a common bird in local woodlots, barred owls started to decline about three decades ago. Finding a barred owl's nest at that time was described as an "extremely rare experience". These owls prefer to nest in tree cavities, and the cutting of

Barred Owls

Barred Owl

39

large trees had reduced the availability of such sites. Three naturalists, Cyril Coldwell, Mark Elderkin and Bernard Forsythe, recognized the problem and launched a programme to erect owl boxes, for the barred owl can be enticed to nest in a box. They placed owl boxes, with permission, in a number of local woodlots. Over several years, Bernard put up twenty-five boxes and in one recent season owls successfully raised young in fifteen of them.

Today, barred owls are one of our most common birds of prey. The nest-box programme provided the needed nesting sites. Also of importance, the programme generated considerable public interest in owls, and the "owl prowl" became one of the more popular field trips offered each spring by our naturalists society.

Bald Eagles

Bald eagles come to The Old Place in winter and perch in the elm trees along the river and sail over the dyked fields on their way to and from the tidal flats. Near noon, when the sun is strong enough to create rising columns of warm air, called thermals, the eagles soar high above the fields and interact with one another and with ravens. At night, they fly into ravines on the side of the mountain where they roost in the shelter of coniferous trees and from where, in the morning, they have a view across the dykelands.

The story of the local population of bald eagles is an excellent example of how naturalists, scientists, individuals and communities worked together to help a population recover. Eagles were scarce in this area in the mid 1900s, but today we have a healthy and expanding population. While discontinuing use of pesticides like DDT was a critical factor, a change in human attitudes was another reason for the eagle recovery. Attitudes gained from the pleasure and excitement of watching these magnificent birds replaced those that once led to killing them and destroying their nests.

The provision of winter feeding stations is another explanation for the growth of the eagle population. Farm carrion is a valuable source of energy. In the early 1960s, Cyril Coldwell, a local farmer and birder, established a carrion pile on his farm and after several years up to fifty eagles sometimes visited it at one time. Other farmers followed his example, as did fish-processing

Bald Eagle

plants along the coast. One poultry farmer, Dick Harvey, described the arrangement as: "a good partnership. The eagles need to eat and I have mortality in my barn. They clean it up."

While eagles of all ages visit these sites, feeding stations are especially helpful to young birds that are inexperienced in the techniques of foraging during the difficult winter period. Researchers have shown that only 63% of eaglets survive the first year, and that this increases to 73% when winter feeding stations are available. Survival of second-year birds shows a similar improvement.

Eagle: 2nd Winter

One day each winter, local naturalists conduct an eagle count. Teams of observers located in different areas record all eagles seen during an agreed one-hour period. In the late 1970s the counts were in the thirty-to-forty range. Today (1997) they are in the 500 range. However, the increase in numbers is only part of the story. For many years, the counts were predominantly of adult birds. Now there are also good numbers of immature birds, meaning that more young are surviving the early years and will enter the breeding population. Unquestionably, winter feeding stations are a major contributor to the recovery and continuing expansion of the local eagle population.

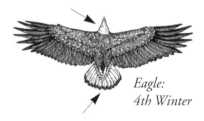

Eagle: 4th Winter

Winter feeding stations are ideal places to watch eagles. They have converted many people into "eagle-watchers" and helped change human attitudes toward these birds and other wildlife. Eagles display a number of interesting and curious behaviours. One interaction is a call described as "peeting", a series of high-pitched notes. It is often accompanied by "head-tossing" and usually is uttered as a "greeting" when a second eagle approaches the perch. When threatened, the eagle utters a series of shrill "screams".

Many interactions are associated with obtaining food. Eagles steal food from one another. One eagle may fly above another with food, harass it until it drops the food, and then catch the food as it falls. Alternatively, an eagle may fly up under one with food, roll over, and reach up with its talons to grab the food. Adult eagles also chase ravens with food, and ravens chase and steal food from immature eagles.

Beginning in January, pairs of eagles soar high and per-

"Cartwheels"

form a number of graceful and acrobatic manoeuvres, with swooping and roll-over flight patterns. Most excitingly, as breeding time approaches, pairs sometimes lock talons and engage in a series of aerial cartwheels. Eagles mate for life if they are successful in producing young, and soaring is part of their yearly courtship behaviour to renew this bond.

Each February, Sheffield Mills, a neighbouring community, organizes an "Eagle-Watch Weekend" and invites everyone to come and enjoy the birds. The weekend's activities are centred at the Community Hall, where breakfast and hot refreshments are served, crafts sold, and videos of local eagles and hawks shown. Maps of the area showing eagle sites are available, the farmers give people permission to enter their properties, and naturalists to answer questions are present at the viewing sites. About 3000 people come, and there may be 250 to 300 eagles about the community. It is an exciting weekend with much to see, both indoors and out.

Helping Others

We now have a healthy eagle population and are able to help other areas re-establish theirs. In the early 1980s Nova Scotian scientists and United States wildlife officials launched a programme to re-establish eagles in southern New England. Over a six-year period, forty eaglets from Nova Scotia, and others from elsewhere, were translocated to artificial nests in the north-eastern United States. These eaglets did remarkably well, and in 1989 the first nest in Massachusetts in eighty years produced two eaglets. By 1993, there were nine resident pairs in Massachusetts and Connecticut. The bald eagle has now been removed from the list of endangered species in those states.

Local Stewardship

Many individuals and communities support projects in wildlife stewardship. Locally, because naturalists recognized the problems and provided leadership, and with the continuing work of interested individuals and entire communities, people today are able to enjoy watching owls, bald eagles and other wildlife. "Let the eagle be your guide to go further than you can see" (Mi'kmaq lore) might well be the slogan for community stewardship groups.

THE RIVER GARDEN

"A small river or stream flowing by one's door has many attractions…
One can make a companion of it; he can walk with it and sit with it,
or lounge on its banks, and feel that it is all his own."

Signs and Seasons
John Burroughs, 1886

A RIVER AND A VILLAGE

The European settlers first dyked the river and converted the tidal marshes into productive fields, where they grew crops, cut hay and pastured livestock. Today, with the prospect of sea levels rising as a result of climatic warming, we will have to relearn the art of building dykes to protect coastal communities and crop lands from flooding. The techniques of the early settlers will be especially useful to less developed countries, which lack the engineering resources available to industralized nations.

The Early Days

Like many communities, the village in which we live grew on the shores of a river. The Habitant River flows along the southeast border of The Old Place and continues eastward past the village to the Minas Basin. It begins several kilometres to the west from small brooks on the mountain and marshes on the lowlands. Geologically, the swift current of the young river helped shape the valley and, starting about 5000 years ago as the tides grew in height, the tidal marshes were formed by sediment deposited when the water overflowed its banks. Now a mature river, it meanders widely between the uplands as it flows eastward. Historically, the story of the village is centred on the river.

Three hundred years ago, the Habitant River was a channel draining the Habitant Creek, an expansive tidal flat of about seven kilometres in length by one-half kilometre in width. It was flooded every twelve hours and twenty-five minutes by the high tide. Before the European settlers arrived, the Mi'kmaq people had a summer camp on the bank overlooking the creek. From there, they launched their canoes and were quickly carried by the tides to fish on the Minas Basin and to collect shellfish on the tidal marshes. Fishing became a major industry after the European settlers established their homesteads. They brought their catches up the river and landed them on the shore about a half kilometre below The Old Place. There, they split the fish and placed them on racks to dry in the sun.

During the late 1600s and 1700s, the French and later the English settlers built dykes along either side of the river to stop the flooding and claimed the marsh for pasture and hay land. The dyke wall was about one-and-a-half metres high. Heavy equipment is now used to build and maintain dykes, but the first dykes were built primarily with power provided by the workers. A narrow trench was first dug along the path of the proposed dyke, and a "keel" along the base of the wall fitted into it. This anchored the dyke and prevented the rising tide from pushing it out over the slippery mud. The wall was constructed of marsh clay and surfaced with bricks of sod. This sod was cut with a specially squared "dyking" spade, for the sides of the bricks had to fit tightly to prevent water from seeping in and eroding the core of the wall. Where available, the sods were cut in patches of black grass, a tidal-marsh rush, because its roots formed deep networks and tightly bound the clay.

Dyking could be done only at low tide, and the challenge was to complete a small section and close it off before the water rose again. Later, between tides, the section was gradually extended along the river. Where exposed to the sea, the dykes were reinforced with planks and rocks, and with a heavy framework of logs and brush when built across river beds.

To drain the dyked fields, aboiteaux or sluice-ways were placed in stream beds and buried in the dyke. The first aboiteaux were simply hollow logs, each with a hinged gate designed so that it would open at low tide and allow the fresh water to escape, and be pushed closed by the rising tide to keep out the salt water. Later, after sawmills were built, these sluices were made of squared timbers, often of oak. Today, they are made of steel.

It required two or three years for the rain to wash the salt from the soil. During this time, the dyked land was used for pasturage and haying. The first major crops were wheat and peas. Other grains were also grown as were cabbage and turnip. One popular winter soup was made of cabbage, turnip and pork.

Later, these early dykes were replaced by others built by people working with drags and teams of horses, but the design was basically the same. Thus, more than a hundred years later when The Old Place was built, the tide flowed up the Habitant River

Dykes and Aboiteaux

Dyke

Aboiteau open

Aboiteau closed

twice a day, but the dykes protected the fields from flooding with salt water.

Prosperous Community

Schooner

The community grew into a prosperous town during the 1800s, with a population four times larger than the present one. Farms expanded on the uplands and extended down to include the pasture and hay lands protected by the dykes along the river. Wharves were constructed behind the business section where coastal ships were loaded with produce from the farms. An axe factory was built, also located beside the river so that ships could unload the coal and coke needed to heat the forges. It continued to produce axes until the 1930s. Construction of wooden ships began in the early 1800s and became a flourishing industry with at least three shipyards in the community by 1850. One of the shipyards was located adjacent to The Old Place. Two- and three-masted schooners rigged fore-and-aft were built, as well as two-masted brigantines rigged with a square sail on the foremast and fore-and-aft on the main mast. They were beautiful ships with full-blown sails. The last wooden ship, the *Fieldwood*, was launched in 1920. She was a tern, a three-masted schooner, and was lost off Sable Island in 1938.

In the mid 1800s, a dam was built across the Habitant River about fifty metres downstream from The Old Place. It contained a large aboiteau that prevented the salt water from flowing upstream. After its construction, the dykes running along the sides of the river above the dam deteriorated, and large sections were deliberately broken down and ploughed back into the fields. The tide continued to rise and fall below the aboiteau, but upstream the river filled with fresh water.

The Flood

This dam and aboiteau broke in September 1944. A wall of salt water surged through the opening into the Habitant River, flowed over its banks and flooded the hay fields of the original tidal marsh to the depth of a metre. The flooding continued twice each day until a new dam and aboiteau were built. The fields at The Old Place were again submerged and the water flowed up to the foot of the lawn. The salt water killed the plant life, including a productive orchard of apple trees that had been planted on the meadow.

In 1945 a new dam-aboiteau was constructed downstream from the village, and replaced in 1978 when it started to leak. The last one was equipped with heavy coffers of sheet steel to protect the three sluice-ways that make up the aboiteau. With construction of these dams, the tide no longer flowed to the village, ships could no longer sail upstream, and the wharf was allowed to deteriorate.

Today

The Habitant River where it flows past The Old Place is now essentially a freshwater river, although a thin layer of salt water seeps through the aboiteau and lies on the bottom. The river bed is one of deep clay and sand typical of the neighbouring marshes, and many plants along the river are species that are also found on the upper regions of the marshes. A ten-metre section of the old dyke still remains, but is now used only as a comfortable perch from which we watch the birds and other wildlife on the river. Downstream, a family of kingfishers nests in the bank of the washed-out dam, and cormorants dive for food among the pilings of the old wharf.

Natural History and Community History

Interests in natural history and community history complement one another, for people are a part of nature. Changes in land use, including draining marshes, altering water courses, cutting forests and cultivating land, are practices that have influenced the present flora and fauna about our communities. A knowledge of community history helps explain our present natural history. It also provides the longer term view needed to intrepret many of the ongoing changes that we now observe.

BIRDING THE RIVER

Several factors have influenced shorebird and waterfowl populations through the years. Unremitting hunting and egg collecting had profound effects, but are now controlled. Changes in land use, including drainage of wetlands and water pollution, have been and continue to be major influences. Communities and land owners can help. They can establish protected areas, restore wetlands and reduce water pollution. Collectively, such actions will help provide the habitat needed to ensure the continued well-being of these birds.

A variety of shorebirds and waterfowl visit the Habitant River each year, some for a brief period during migration and others to nest. A comparison of bird lists recorded during the past few decades shows that some species are becoming more abundant, that others are fairly recent arrivals, and that both trends are continuing. This is in contrast to reports of a hundred and more years ago that record the decimation of entire populations. The present trends illustrate the need to protect birds, and emphasize the value of recent efforts to maintain and restore wetlands.

Diving Birds

The first birds to arrive on the river each spring are common mergansers and common goldeneyes. Both species are relative newcomers to this area. Bird lists prepared seventy-five years ago do not include the goldeneye and describe the merganser as an "uncommon winter visitor". Locally, both species are now present in winter in sites of open fresh water, and move to the Habitant River when the ice starts to break up in March. They visit for only a few weeks and then move elsewhere to nest.

Mergansers and goldeneyes are diving ducks. A good population of small fish and invertebrates lives in the river and these birds feed on them. The merganser's bill has saw-toothed edges and a hooked tip, both adaptations that help them catch and hold fish while swimming under water.

The goldeneyes dive for insect larvae and other invertebrates that are abundant on aquatic plants and the river bottom. They likely catch small eels as well. The males have a white patch

Common Merganser

48

just behind the bill that is a good identification aid. Goldeneyes are so-named because they have bright yellow eyes. They are also called "whistlers" because their rapid wing beats often make a clear, whistling sound, although they can fly quietly. Some authorities believe the birds maintain contact with one another by means of this whistling. Downstream, where the old dam washed out, the rocks and swift current create a short rapids. The goldeneyes play there. They fly upstream, drift down either frontwards or backwards, and dive just as they enter the rapids. They emerge again in the smoother water downstream, rest for a few moments, and then fly up the river and dive again. On much larger rivers, we have watched goldeneyes "shooting the rapids" for distances of up to fifty metres.

Goldeneye

Another diving bird that returns to the river in late March is the double-crested cormorant. Cormorants are large black birds that have an orange pouch beneath their bills. This pouch is featherless and expandable, although not to the size that the pelicans, their relatives, can expand theirs. We see three or four cormorants during most walks along the river in summer and autumn, and occasionally birds remain until freeze-up in December. They swim low in the water, with head and bill tilted upwards, and dive repeatedly to pursue and catch eels and other fish. They perch on the pilings of the old wharf with wings held out to dry.

The size of the cormorant population has varied considerably since the arrival of the first settlers. Reports indicate that cormorants were numerous along the Nova Scotian coast at that time, although their nesting colonies were scattered. In 1604 Samuel de Champlain visited the "Isle of Cormorants" off the southern end of Nova Scotia, "so-named because of the infinite number of these birds, of whose eggs we took a barrel full". In 1610, in the same area, a party led by Monsieur de Potrincourt became lost and was able to survive by roasting and eating cormorants. During the 1700s and early 1800s, cormorants were shot and trapped, eggs collected, young captured and nests destroyed. Some cormorants, especially the young, were eaten and others were used to bait fishing (mainly cod) lines. Most were used for food on fox farms and to feed dogs. The eggs were used in cooking and were considered "very strengthening to the stomach".

Cormorant

Cormorant numbers dropped dramatically as colonies were destroyed or abandoned and, by the mid 1800s, they were described as "not common". Locally, we have records of two specimens collected in 1917, and they appear to be the only ones for the years around the turn of the century. Possibly, cormorants were not present on the Habitant River when The Old Place was built. Their numbers remained low for the first half of the 1900s, but increased in the 1940s and were described as "locally common" in reports written in the 1950s. Cormorants underwent a major population expansion during the 1970s and are now common along the entire coast. During the late 1960s, they established a breeding colony on an island across the Basin from The Old Place, and about 200 pairs now nest there. They share this island with great blue herons, herring gulls and great black-backed gulls.

Surface Feeders

Several species of surface-feeding ducks, or marsh ducks, are resident on the river and others visit occasionally. We see black ducks during most walks in summer, and the loud "quacks" of the females and softer "reeps" of the males are familiar sounds as they swim along the shore and tip to feed on aquatic plants and animals. Black ducks nest in April and early May. They do not nest along the river, but we have found their nests in hedgerows and woodlots sometimes located a kilometre away. In mid summer, we sometimes see one or two hens leading their broods across the meadow toward the river, and clusters of ducklings are on the river in early August.

Black Duck

Green-winged and blue-winged teals arrive in April, with the green-wings returning first, and remain until mid autumn. Both nest along the river, and some years we see two flotillas of young blue-wings swimming behind their mothers about the reeds. Mallards are recent additions. Our first sighting was in August 1983, when we saw a mother and seven young. They are now common throughout the area. One or two American wigeons stop during spring and fall migrations and, occasionally a bufflehead visits. The white head-patch of the bufflehead is especially striking against the dark waters of early spring.

Several shorebirds visit the river through the seasons, including great blue herons; least, semipalmated and spotted sandpipers; greater and lesser yellowlegs; willets; common snipe and short-billed dowitchers.

Herons arrive in late March and remain until the water freezes in December. We see them during most walks in summer. Sometimes herons fly in from the Basin and glide gracefully down to alight in the reeds. At other times, they approach from over the trees and the drop requires the bird to tilt awkwardly from side to side, with its long legs dangling, as it parachutes down into the water. Herons slowly stalk their prey or stand quietly and wait for it to come within reach, and then lunge to grab it with their sword-like bill. About forty pairs of herons nest in trees on an island in the Basin. Some authorities believe that birds in nesting colonies exchange information about good foraging sites, or simply follow one another. This improves their chances of finding an adequate food supply during the critical nesting period.

A related species, the little blue heron, visited the river a short distance below The Old Place in late October 1986. However, it remained downstream and we were unable to add its name to our list of birds seen on the property. We had better luck with other related species: a snowy egret that glided down across the meadow in April 1980 to alight beside a neighbouring pond, a great egret that spent a few weeks on the river in August 1992, and a black-crowned night-heron that perched in an elm tree overlooking the river one May morning in 1996.

The loud, plaintive, three-note calls of the greater yellowlegs announce their return in mid April. Before we reach the river on our morning walk, we can hear them calling from the shore, or see them flying in tight circles over the fields while calling loudly. Their habit of "bobbing" their tails while foraging makes them easy to recognize. Yellowlegs leave for their nesting sites in northern Nova Scotia, Newfoundland and Labrador during the latter half of May, although some may migrate further west. However, they return in mid August, and lesser yellowlegs join them in September. The two species forage together and give us a good opportunity to compare sizes and calls: the lesser is smaller and often utters a weaker, one or two-note call.

Shorebirds

Great Blue Heron

Yellowleg

Sometimes, in autumn, there are as many as eight yellowlegs along the river and fifteen to twenty calling loudly overhead as they fly between the Basin and neighbouring farm ponds.

From late July through September, flocks of up to a hundred short-billed dowitchers visit the river and adjacent ponds. Most dowitchers migrate north through the central provinces and nest in northern Canada, and those in the east move to the Atlantic coast after nesting. While numerous now, dowitchers were scarce in the early 1900s and did not become a regular migrant to this area until the late 1930s. Once heavily hunted, shorebird numbers started to increase after approval of the Migratory Bird Convention Act in 1917. With this protection, the ranges of several shorebirds, including dowitchers, expanded along the Atlantic coast.

Dowitcher

We were greeted by a willet during our morning walk on May 2, 1980. It was a welcomed sighting, a new species for the property list. We had just crossed the field when we heard the loud "pill-will-willet" and saw the large shorebird, with black and white wings, darting about and scolding our intrusion. Willets were rarely seen in this area a few decades ago. They were once common along the Atlantic shore of Nova Scotia, but the population was reduced by hunting. They arrived on this side of the Minas Basin in the early 1970s, but rarely flew inland along the rivers. We have seen others along the Habitant River since that first sighting, and hope that their range continues to expand and that they will soon be regular visitors to the garden.

Since that first sighting, in June 1984 we found a willet's nest on the upper tidal marsh about three kilometres below The Old Place. It contained four eggs and, curiously, was located only thirty-four centimetres from a gray partridge's nest that contained nineteen eggs. It was a good illustration of the fact that two species may nest close together without aggression.

Willet

Population Changes

The numbers of shorebirds and waterfowl have undergone dramatic changes during the past century and a half. Some species have increased in numbers, their ranges have expanded and they have become regular visitors to The Old Place. This trend continues today. On the other hand, Labrador ducks were once present on the rocky shores only a few kilometres away. While not numerous, they were hunted for market and for private and museum collections. Eskimo curlews were also plentiful at one time on the tidal shores during autumn migration and, here as elsewhere, were hunted in enormous numbers. Harlequin ducks once occurred regularly on the Minas Basin, although a sighting now is unusual. They were known as the Lords and Ladies of the Sea because of their strikingly coloured plumage, although hunters called them Lords and Imps because they were so difficult to shoot. Today, Labrador ducks are extinct, Eskimo curlews are very near extinction, and the Atlantic population of harlequins has declined to the point that recently they were added to the list of endangered species.

Healthy populations of shorebirds and waterfowl require wetlands, clean feeding areas, undisturbed nesting sites and preserves where hunting is not permitted. Locally, land owners and communities can provide these requirements. Land owners, independently and in groups, can formally place land in conservation programmes, or can simple allow it to remain undisturbed. Has your community established wildlife conservation areas? A positive conservation ethic must be a part of community planning. It is best provided by local naturalists.

Community Wildlife Preserves

CANOEING THE RIVER

A river is a valuable ecosystem, it is not a waste disposal unit. Pollution is usually the result of ignorance, carelessness and lack of interest, for the needed technologies are available. A healthy river with wildlife is a place of aesthetic, educational and, with care, recreational values. Communities and land owners have the first responsibility to keep the water clean, to allow the river to be "wild".

Photographs of the Canning harbour taken in the early 1900s show as many as eleven sailing ships lined up at high tide waiting their turn to tie up at the wharf. They were wooden ships in the 150 tonne range. Many were loaded with apples and potatoes, hauled to the wharf in wagons pulled by teams of oxen. Today, however, with new aboiteau gates to control the water level, the river is best navigated by canoe.

It is pleasant to paddle and drift along the river in the evening, with the colours of the setting sun mirrored in the water. There are many plants and animals to look for: schools of small fish dart among the aquatic plants, black ducks and teal dabble within the beds of pickerelweed, one or two herons cautiously stalk prey among the reeds with their images perfectly reflected by the water, and swallows skim over the water hawking for insects and dipping for a drink. Occasionally we flush a bittern, an awkward looking bird until it collects its dangling legs. Once in flight, however, its long beak and black mustache give it a determined expression.

Amphibians

The canoeing season begins in early May when the amphibians start calling. We can find several species by drifting along the shore on a warm evening, and especially after a soft rain. The long rattles and chuckles of leopard frogs are easy to recognize, as are the high trills of toads. Later in the season, the "jug-o-rums" of bullfrogs come from the sandy delta where the drains from the field empty into the river. Once the amphibians start calling, the next challenge is to find them. They are most vocal in late evening and a flashlight is helpful. Some amphibians ignore us and sit among the reeds and grasses with only their heads above water, others breaststroke from one patch of reeds to hide in another, and most simply dive but come up nearby within a few moments if we wait quietly.

In many places, the numbers of amphibians have undergone dramatic reductions during the past decade. Practices such as draining marshes and meadows, and cutting forests often result in a loss of amphibian habitat. Acid rain and other types of pollution also reduce breeding success. Amphibians live both on land and in water. They have a moist, permeable skin and quickly respond to changes in the quality of the air and water. Amphibian populations are excellent indicators of environmental stress and should be monitored with care. Healthy amphibian populations mean healthy ecosystems that can support a variety of living things. Community "frogwatch" programmes are very popular and provide useful information.

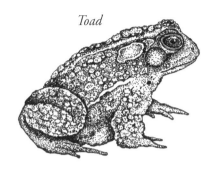

Toad

Fish

Local people fish the river for brook trout. Although we do not fish, we enjoy the quiet time with nature and, like those who do, we anxiously watch for trout to break water. Eels are abundant in the river, creek chubs and white suckers are also present as are three- and four-spined sticklebacks, and schools of banded killifish dart about the aquatic plants causing ripples to spread across the water.

Brook or speckled trout are most active in spring and autumn. Their season begins in April when their colours are best: dark green backs with wavy lines, cream-coloured bellies, red and yellow spots outlined with blue, and white-edged fins. Most of the spring trout are sea-run fish and may weigh up to half a kilogram.

Brook trout move downstream to deeper water with the warmer temperatures of summer, and return to The Old Place when the temperatures cool in autumn. They do not spawn here, for the silt carried by the water would smother their eggs. Rather, in October and November, they move up to the clear, cooler waters of the streams at the base of the mountain where they inhabit the well-oxygenated pools below rapids and waterfalls. Their scientific name describes this preference: *fontinalis* means "a

Brook Trout

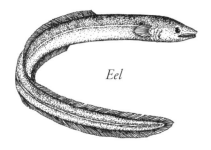

Eel

dweller in springs and fountains". There, the spawning trout hollow out their redds in the beds of clean gravel and shed their eggs. The eggs remain in the gravel over winter and hatch in spring.

One highlight of spring on the river is the eel migration. Not everyone realizes that many animals other than birds follow migration routes that are long and complex. The American eel is one of them. While several species of fish move from the sea to spawn in freshwater rivers and lakes, the eel is the only local fish that migrates from fresh water to spawn in the sea. When mature, at seven to nine years of age, eels in eastern North America (and western Europe) migrate to the warm, highly saline currents of the Sargasso Sea, near Bermuda. There they spawn and die.

The eggs hatch and the transparent larvae begin their migration to the coast of Nova Scotia, finding their way without parental guidance. It takes about a year for them to reach Nova Scotia. By the time they arrive in spring, they have grown to a length of about seven centimetres. The young eels, or "elvers", are greenish-brown and enter the rivers in enormous numbers. On some evenings in May, the surface of the water about our canoe "boils" as successive schools of elvers swarm upstream.

Three-spined sticklebacks are common in the river. They grow to about eight centimetres in length and have three movable, sharp spines on their backs. They are usually gray to greenish-brown, but are more brightly coloured at spawning time in June and July. Then the males have bluish backs and red bellies, and the females are a camouflaged brown with pink underparts. The males construct nests by sticking together small twigs and bits of vegetation, and the females lay their eggs in them. The nests are easier to find after the eggs are laid because the males stay nearby to protect both eggs and young from predators. Males also aerate the eggs at regular intervals by fanning water over them with their fins.

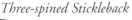

Three-spined Stickleback

Aquatic Plants

Pickerelweed grows along either side of the river and forms wide borders of blue flowers in summer. It is rooted in the mud, but long stalks reach the surface. The stalks have small air pockets inside them that help the leaves and flowers float upright. The leaves are large, heart-shaped and glossy green. Pickerelweed blossoms in late July and August. Each inflorescence is formed of many blue flowers clustered along a spike, and resembles a hyacinth. Only a few flowers open at a time, and each lasts for just one day after which it closes and the seeds start to form. Thus, the spike supports a mixture of young buds, open flowers, and developing seed capsules. The seeds are a favourite food of waterfowl.

Black ducks and teal moult their feathers during August and are unable to fly. At this time they seek the shelter of the pickerelweed and other plants growing along the bank. There they can hide and find a good supply of food. All birds moult to replace worn feathers, but most replace their flight feathers one at a time and retain the ability to fly. Ducks are different and shed all flight feathers at the same time, and are unable to fly until the new feathers have grown. We can approach them easily at such times by allowing our canoe to drift along the beds of pickerelweed, but the ducks scamper away if we get too close.

Arrowhead is another plant that grows in the water. Its large, shiny leaves, many shaped like arrowheads, are characteristic. It flowers during the latter half of summer and clusters of arrowheads form white islands in the river. The individual flowers are arranged in whorls of three on a tall spire. Wildlife quickly eat the seeds and muskrats collect the corms, or "wild potatoes", and store them in their tunnels.

Muskrats are in the river most evenings and early mornings searching for food. They do not build lodges on our part of the river, but tunnel into the river bank. The entrances are under water, usually hidden among the reeds and lead to nesting chambers located in the bank above water level. The young are born in summer and often we see the adults carrying grass and roots toward the bank where they dive, presumably to enter a tunnel and take the food to their young. During evenings in early autumn, there may be a family group of four or five muskrats swimming in the river. They do not mind the canoe and we can drift along nearby.

A river can be an attractive place and many pleasant hours may be spent exploring it. A healthy river promotes a diversity of living things. However, its attractiveness is easily lost.

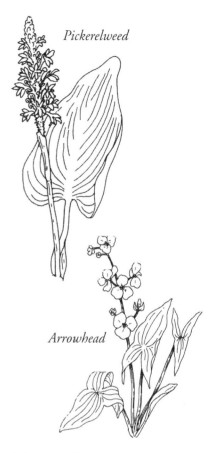

Pickerelweed

Arrowhead

Mammals

Community Asset

Communities must gain a better awareness of river systems, and a determination to maintain their river in a healthy state. An attractive river is a community asset.

THE RIVER BANK

Many plants and animals live on a river bank, and some require both aqueous and terrestrial environments for feeding, shelter and reproduction. However, river banks are fragile systems that are easily damaged. Construction, dumping waste, cultivation, grazing livestock and cutting trees are abuses frequently observed. An undisturbed border is a requirement of a healthy river. Communities and land owners can protect river banks and help maintain these valuable habitats.

The river bank along the Habitant River is the wall of the original channel that once drained the tidal marsh and filled and emptied twice each day with the rising and ebbing of the tide. Today, with a dam and aboiteau downstream to block the tide, the river contains much less water and a high, sloping bank is exposed.

Vegetation

Grasses, herbs and scattered bushes and trees cover the bank. The slender stocks and leaves of meadow fescue surface the upper bank. It is a common forage grass grown on the dykelands. Broad-leaf cordgrass covers the lower bank and extends into the water. Other local cordgrasses grow only on the tidal marsh, but broad-leaf also grows along adjacent freshwater rivers and on wet meadows.

Broad-leaf is the tallest of the local cordgrasses and may grow to more than a metre in height. It has upright stems and long, narrow leaves. The spikelets of flowers appear in July, and release pollen in such large quantities that it coats the water with a yellow film. Broad-leaf has an extensive network of rhizomes and roots that firmly anchors the soils of the lower bank. This limits erosion and reduces the amount of sediment that enters the water.

Along the shore, this cordgrass forms a dense border that provides an important zone where wildlife can forage and seek shelter from predators. It also produces large volumes of nutrients that disperse downstream and contribute to the high productivity of the estuary. The early farmers recognized this rich nutrient quality and cut broad-leaf to feed livestock, and today a patch of

Broad-leaf Cordgrass

this cordgrass on a meadow is the first choice of cattle and horses at pasture.

Mammals

Racoon Tracks

Several small mammals live on the river bank. Meadow voles and short-tailed shrews are common there, as they are on the meadow generally. Raccoons come down to the river at night to rummage along the shore. In the morning, their long-toed tracks in the mud show where they were the night before. Occasionally we see a mink, but not very often for they are primarily nocturnal animals. More frequently we see their tracks in the mud, again showing that they were active at night. Mink travel from the river bank to hunt over the dykelands and, from time to time, we see one bounding across the lawn. Mink are expert mousers. They are also excellent swimmers and catch fish and other underwater animals

Shorebirds

Spotted Sandpiper in Winter Plumage

Spotted sandpipers are present in summer and we see them during most walks along the river bank. They are one of only a few shorebirds that nest there. Spotted sandpipers return in mid May, still with the unspotted breasts of their winter plumage. They search among the grasses for insects, worms and other small animals. The spotted sandpiper is one of the shorebirds that "teeters" its tail, and this habit is a good identification aid as is its clear, repeated, "peet-weet" call. Its flight pattern is also distinctive. The wings curve downward and the wing beats are very shallow, not lifting above the horizontal. Spotted sandpipers nest under the bushes on the bank. The nest is little more than a depression in the ground. It is the male bird that incubates the eggs and cares for the young. Sometimes in late June and early July, we see the young scampering through the vegetation after their father.

Pleasantly Singing Song-finch

Song sparrows are present on all parts of the property. However, we associate them mainly with the river bank because they are always there in summer and several remain in the shelter of its thickets in winter. In late March, regardless of weather or temperature, a song sparrow perches on top of a rose bush and, with head held upward, diligently announces the arrival of spring.

Song sparrows sing continuously throughout the summer months, and with most enthusiasm during the morning and evening. This makes them a favourite companion on walks and while working in the garden. They sing during the rest of the year as well, including a cheerful song from time to time in mid winter, but not as frequently as in spring. They also utter "tchep" notes when flitting through bushes. These are contact notes that help keep the pair or family together.

Song Sparrow

Their scientific name, *Melospiza melodia*, means a "pleasantly singing song-finch". The typical song consists of three to five phrases, usually including several, clear, introductory notes and at least one trill. In spring the songs may be sung several times per minute. Each male develops five or six songs for his repertoire, which is sufficiently distinctive that researchers can recognize individual birds by listening to their songs. The males usually sing from a few selected perches within their territories, often from a post or the uppermost branch of a low shrub or small tree. The males sing to establish territories and keep away intruders, and to attract mates. They probably also sing as a means of socializing and perhaps just for the pure enjoyment of singing. The adults teach the song-types to their young and much of the singing in the early summer is for that purpose. Although the ability to sing is inherent, the young must hear the adults to learn the "song sparrow" songs and they must practise to refine their singing talents.

Redwings

Red-winged blackbirds are one of the first songbirds to return each spring. Twenty to thirty redwings arrive during the latter half of March. They live among the reeds on the river bank where they pull cattail heads apart and eat the numerous moth larvae that live within them. At first, the redwings fly back and forth between the river and a neighbouring farm pond that has a larger cattail marsh than the one along the river. Redwings nest in colonies and remain at the pond once the ice has melted in late April. There they establish their territories and begin nesting. While their stay at the river is a brief one, the redwings are a welcome reminder that spring has arrived, and they do remain long enough to show some of their interesting patterns of behaviour.

The male redwings arrive first. They are black with scarlet

shoulder-patches or epaulettes and are very conspicuous against the brown reeds and patches of snow. They arrive quietly, but within a few days their "a-ree" and "onk-a-ree" calls again become familiar sounds. The scarlet patches may be flared and in striking contrast to the black body, or they may be drawn under other feathers and be inconspicuous when the bird conceals itself in reeds and bushes. At such times, only a yellowish line across the shoulder is visible and confirms the identification.

Several redwings take up temporary residence among the river cattails. We watch them from the bank and pick out one male and try to follow him. He sings from a cluster of cattails, with his epaulettes flared and wings and tail spread. He then flies to other perches and repeats the display. Redwings defend these temporary sites. They chase redwings and other birds away and scold, flick their tails angrily and dive at intruders, including birders who walk down among the cattails. When they move to the pond, they define and maintain their nesting territories in the same way.

Redwings

The female redwings usually arrive a week or more after the males. They are brown and heavily streaked, typical of the camouflage colouration shown by many birds that nest in reeds. The males sing and display with more enthusiasm after the females arrive, and many of their courtship and pair-formation activities begin along the river. The male chases a female, or hovers over her, chatters loudly and displays his epaulettes. As courtship progresses, he struts about on the ground, periodically crouching with bill pointed upward, and displays spread wings and shoulder-patches. The female responds by singing and fluffing out her feathers (the female redwing is one of the few female songbirds that sings). Many of these interactions are typical of those exhibited later on their nesting territories around the pond.

After nesting, redwings form flocks and wander widely, and thirty or forty are sometimes present on the river bank in mid September. Redwings begin to leave in early October to winter in the southern United States. However, a few spend the winter here, in neighbouring orchards and hedgerows where they feed on left-over fruit and weed seeds, and several are regular visitors to our bird feeders. Their epaulettes are often concealed in winter, but when displayed the scarlet gives a colourful contrast against the snow.

There is a high bank about thirty metres downstream from The Old Place, the remains of the old dam and aboiteau that washed out in 1944. A pair of kingfishers lives there. The male has a blue band across his breast and the female has two bands, one blue and the other reddish. One often perches in a tree beside the old dam. When a fish comes near the surface, it plunges into the water to catch it. Kingfishers have bifocal vision, with one type used in the air and the other while under water.

The scientific name for the kingfisher is *alcyon*. In mythology, Alcyon or Halcyone was the wife of Ceyx. She drowned herself when Ceyx was lost at sea and the gods turned both Alcyone and Ceyx into kingfishers. The gods also forbade the winds to blow during the winter solstice, the period when the kingfishers nested. Thus, this time became known as "the halcyon days", a time of peace and tranquillity. "Halcyon" might also describe the river bank, except the tranquillity is regularly shattered by the loud, rattle-like calls that the kingfishers utter during their frequent patrols.

These kingfishers nest in a burrow in the old dam. They chisel out the burrow with their bills while scratching the soil back with their feet. We see the young looking out of their burrow in late June. They fly within a few days and join the rest of us on the river bank.

An intact bank is an essential part of a healthy river ecosystem. It is home to many species of plants and animals. A disturbed river bank usually results in loss of soil from adjacent fields and forest floors, adding sediment to the water and making the river unsuitable for many plants and animals. The vegetation on the bank provides an important source of nutrients for the river. In wooded areas, the shade from trees reduces variation in water temperature and helps maintain the cooler levels needed by aquatic organisms. Protecting the river bank is an important part of river conservation programmes.

Halcyon Days

Halcyone

River Conservation

DRAGONFLIES AND DAMSELFLIES

A careful study of one group of plants or animals, such as orchids, shorebirds or dragonflies, is an excellent way to become familiar with the complexities of the natural world. It best demonstrates how species relate to their habitats, how they interact with other plants and animals, and how vulnerable they are to environmental degradation. Observations by naturalists have provided much of the information known about many plants and animals.

Dragonflies are plentiful along the river from June through autumn, with peak numbers in July. They alight on the pickerelweed and cordgrass where we can watch them easily with binoculars. Naturalists who study dragonflies and damselflies as a hobby have provided much useful information about their life cycles and patterns of behaviour. Such information has also helped to explain similar behaviours in other animals. Many questions, however, still await answers.

There may be fifty species of dragonflies and damselflies on the river and dykelands, but we have identified only a few of them. The dragonflies are robust insects and fly rapidly; the damselflies are more delicate and fly slowly. Both have two pairs of wings. The dragonflies hold their wings outstretched when at rest, and the hind wings are wider than the front wings. The damselflies fold their wings back, either over the abdomen or turned upward, and their front and back wings are the same size. As major predators on mosquitoes and blackflies, both dragonflies and damselflies are welcome inhabitants of the river.

Dragonflies and damselflies must live near water. The local species lay their eggs in water and the larval or nymph forms live in water. The nymph stages make up the longest part of their life cycle. The nymphs are voracious feeders and this is a time of growth. This stage may last for two years in some species. In the summer of their second year, usually during the night, the nymphs crawl up the plant stems and out of the water. They shed their exoskeletons, freeing their wings that they hold open for a short time to dry and harden. Then they start to beat their wings rapidly and in a few moments launch into their maiden flight.

Darner

Sometimes there are many cast-off exoskeletons on the water plants because many nymphs emerge at the same time. The adult flying stage is the shorter part of their life cycle. It is the stage for dispersal and reproduction. For some species on the river, it lasts for only two or three weeks.

Darners, clubtails and skimmers are the three different groups of dragonflies. The darners are the largest, measuring up to eight centimetres in length.. They are dark brown, often with blue and green markings. Darners range for considerable distances over the dykelands and adjacent uplands. Clubtails are slightly smaller than darners. Their bodies are also brown, but with yellow and green markings, and the ends of their tails are enlarged or club-like. The skimmers are the smallest of the three groups and measure up to six centimetres in length. They differ from the others in that they have brown or white patches near the ends of their wings, whereas the darners and clubtails have no wing markings. All dragonflies are strong fliers. They are capable of sudden bursts of speed, but can hover and fly forward, backwards and sideways. Dragonflies, unlike many insects, are able to move their wings independently and this might explain their maneuverability.

Some of the large darners, and perhaps other dragonflies, undergo lengthy migrations in autumn and spring. Birders, banding birds in September at the southern tip of Nova Scotia, also catch darners in their mist nets. These dragonflies are flying out across the Gulf of Maine towards New England and destinations unknown. Darners can fly at speeds of up to twenty kilometres per hour, and are also carried by the wind. Where do they go and how far? In spring, large darners appear here before the local populations have emerged. Presumably, these darners migrated here after emerging in more southern locations. The darners that arrive in spring are, of course, not the individuals that left the previous autumn. The life-span of the adult is too short. Thus, the adults of one generation fly south in autumn and those of the next generation come north in spring. Are the spring migrants related to those that migrated south?

It is not known why dragonflies undertake these migrations. Possibly those that fly south are ones that hatched in late

Dragonflies

Clubtail

Skimmer

summer and move to a warmer climate to lay their eggs. Researchers suggest that the migration might be stimulated by factors such as the drying up of ponds, cooler temperatures, shorter daylight hours and the prospect of food shortages. That is, the migration is an attempt to extend the breeding period. The flight north in spring may be undertaken to find new breeding sites. While the real explanations are not known, the migration is a strategy that encourages the dispersal of the species and the colonization of new breeding sites. Observations by local naturalists are a valuable help in answering the questions of where, when and why do dragonflies (and other insects) migrate.

Beautiful
Wings

Damselflies are smaller than most dragonflies, with many measuring less than four centimetres in length, and their bodies are more slender. They come in a variety of vivid colours: some have blue bodies and others are reddish, green, brown or black. Similarly, the wings of some are clear, while those of others are black, gray or brown, and some are colourfully marked. One group of damselflies is commonly known as the broad-wings. Their genus name is *Calopteryx*, from two Greek words that mean, appropriately, "beautiful wings".

Damselfly

One type of broad-wing is numerous about the pickerel-weed and other plants. It is the one we often watch. It has a metallic green body, black legs, and wings marked in such a way that it is possible to distinguish the sexes. It is most abundant in June and early July, and most active in the early afternoon when there is little wind.

Some male damselflies establish territories and defend them. This makes the male damselfly easy to locate and watch. A territory may extend for a distance of several metres along the river. It is centred about a prominent perch, usually a plant stalk that rises above the neighbouring ones, and overlooks a patch of quiet water with submerged plants where the female will lay her eggs. The male flies regular patrols from this perch, usually short trips that follow the same route. During these patrols, the fore and hind wings beat alternately and inscribe a figure "X" pattern, whereas the wings beat synchronously in the usual flight patterns. Possibly, the former provides for greater maneuverability. When another male trespasses into the territory, he is challenged and escorted out by the resident male. Sometimes the interaction is more vigorous, with the two flying in circles and colliding until one retreats. The females do not have a special perch.

Damselflies groom themselves while perched. Their fore legs have special teeth or combs that they brush over their wings and bodies. They then clean the combs by passing them through the mouth or by rubbing the legs together. Damselflies usually fold their wings back when perched, but sometimes splay their wings. That is, they hold their fore wings upward and the hind wings horizontally and slightly rotated. This is the position assumed by newly emerged damselflies while their wings are drying and hardening. Perhaps the adults take this position to absorb the sun's warmth.

When mating, the male and female damselflies form a wheel-like configuration and may remain together for some time. They fly "in tandem" before and after the "wheel" position. The female then begins to lay eggs. She probes a plant with the tip of her abdomen and inserts the eggs, and slowly backs down the plant, probing and depositing eggs until she is completely submerged. The male guards the site from his perch, protecting her from other males, for the process of egg laying may last for an hour or more.

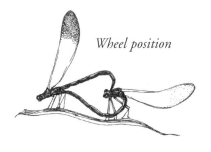

Wheel position

Territories

Establishing a territory has a number of advantages. It is a means of claiming a food supply, protecting a site for egg laying, and guarding the female until she completes egg laying. It also leads to dispersal of the species, for other males are driven away to new areas. Many mammals, birds and other animals establish and defend territories for the same reasons.

Information Needed

Interested naturalists can record much useful information about plant and animal species, as for example: notes on habitats, food preferences, times and patterns of reproduction, behaviours, migrations, dispersals, and associations with other plants and animals. Such information is incomplete and may be lacking for many species. Even for well-studied species, local observations are needed to help describe geographical patterns, for both habits and choices of habitat show interesting variations from region to region. Much of what we know about many plants and animals is based on observations recorded by local naturalists.

WINTER RIVER

Adaptations of behaviour and metabolism permit many river and wetland animals to survive cold temperatures, but in a state that is often near the threshold of death. An unhealthy river reduces the safety margin. Water oxygen is slowly depleted during winter, and organic pollution can reduce it below the levels needed for survival. Infilling from erosion may result in the water freezing down to the river bed, killing the plants and animals that live on the bottom. The river bank provides well-insulated hibernacula, and ground cover and trees for successful foraging and shelter. Clean water and intact river banks are year-round requirements of a healthy river. Both are the responsibility of the neighbouring communities and land owners.

The river freezes in winter. When the ice is smooth we can skate upstream for one or two kilometres, and we can ski when snow covers the ice. The river is at the bottom of the original channel, and the sloping banks on either side provide shelter from the winds that sweep across the dykelands.

Herring and great black-backed gulls sail overhead as they travel between the tidal flats and neighbouring farm fields, but otherwise there appears to be little activity on the river. The swallows that hawked for insects over the water in summer are wintering in the southern States and South America, and the herons and cormorants are in Florida and along the Gulf of Mexico. Four or five song sparrows spend the winter in the shelter of the rose thickets, and occasionally there are juncos and tree sparrows in the reeds nearby.

Herring Gull

Similarly, only a few mammals are in evidence along the river in winter. Muskrats live in their tunnels and chambers in the bank, protected from the cold, and swim under the ice to feed on roots and invertebrates. Star-nosed moles also swim under the ice and feed on insects and other small animals. They have paddle-like feet and large tails and are excellent swimmers. Occasionally we see a mink and rarely a weasel running along the bank and diving into the snow or under a log. A few squeaky noises usually arouse the weasel's curiosity and entice it out from its hiding place so we can have a better look at it.

Red-tails

Hawks are the conspicuous animals along the river in winter. Red-tailed hawks are the most numerous. One or two often perch in the elm trees on the bank or soar high in the rising thermals. They are usually quiet, but sometimes they scream a shrill "kee-er-r-r". We sometimes see rough-legged and sharp-shinned hawks, and occasionally a merlin streaks by or a harrier sails over the meadow.

A few red-tailed hawks nest in this area, but within the seclusion of the woodlands on the mountain and they rarely visit The Old Place in summer. In winter, however, the high numbers of rodents on the farm fields and dykelands attract both local red-tails and those that nested elsewhere. We drive a route of about forty kilometres each week to record wintering eagles and we count red-tails at the same time. On some circuits we have counted as many as seventy red-tails, and seen as many as sixteen perched in one tree.

Red-tailed Hawk

Red-tails hunt while perched and when soaring. They may sit in a tree for hours, scanning the fields for the slightest movement that indicates a rodent. Their eyes, like those of other raptors, are specially adapted for acute vision. Red-tail eyes have about five times the number of visual cells per area of retina as does the human eye. The eyes of all raptors are positioned at the front of the head, rather than on the sides as in other birds. This gives them the binocular vision needed to judge distances accurately, and the ability to "zoom" focus enables the birds to maintain a clear sighting while diving at high speeds.

Edges and clumps of trees are important to the foraging behaviour of red-tails. In the area of The Old Place, agricultural practices have created a mosaic of woodlots, fields and rows of trees. This is an ideal habitat for these birds. Most of their food consists of mice and other small mammals, although they take larger ones when the snow is deep and the vole tunnels buried. We have found red-tails feeding on freshly killed pheasants when skiing along the wooded edges of farm fields. However, they generously repay such losses by their work in controlling the rodent population.

Red-tails soar for long periods over The Old Place. Their broad wings and fanned tails facilitate soaring, as does the topography of the area. The mountain deflects air currents upward and the heat-reflective farm fields create high-rising thermals. Raptors, often accompanied by ravens and gulls, wheel in these updrafts and sometimes reach heights at which they are little more than dark specks. Raptors also travel by riding these updrafts. They soar upward in one air current, then glide down and build up sufficient momentum to carry them to the next updraft. In this way, they travel long distances with little effort.

At night and during inclement weather, red-tails roost in coniferous trees, where they are sheltered by the dense branches. Surviving the cold is a challenge for red-tails, as it is for all plants and animals that live in the north. When temperatures drop, birds must limit loss of heat as well as generate additional heat. Birds begin to acclimatize to the cold in autumn by forming a thick layer of fat under the skin for insulation. They also develop additional feathers, particularly the down feathers next to the skin. These are delicate feathers with many loosely fitting barbs. When "fluffed-out", these feathers interlock and trap a layer of warm air next to the body and form one of the most effective insulations known.

Birds generate additional heat in cold weather by metabolizing greater amounts of fats and carbohydrates. This is done primarily by rapid muscle contraction, or shivering. To produce this extra heat, birds must find more to eat and they congregate wherever a plentiful food supply is available. Curiously, hawks and some other raptors gorge themselves on the day before a storm and then remain in their roost during the storm. How do birds know when a storm is coming? Are they receptive to changes in atmospheric pressure?

While activity above the ice is limited, there is considerable activity under the ice. The water does not freeze down to the river bottom, but ranges from a slushy 1° C just under the ice to 4° C at the bottom. Thus, aquatic animals live at a fairly constant temperature that in mid winter is usually warmer than the temperatures above the ice. The exposed tops of the plants die back, are shorn off by the ice, and carried downstream where they con-

Surviving the Cold

Under the Ice

tribute to the nutrient content of the Basin. However, the roots remain alive in the unfrozen mud and produce new growth in spring.

Many molluscs and other invertebrates are active under the ice, and some aquatic insects breed during the winter. Certain fish, such as mummichogs, burrow into the mud when temperatures drop and hibernate there until the water warms again. Other fish, like trout, move to deeper water where they feed and remain active all winter.

Amphibians

Bullfrog

Leopard Frog

The amphibians illustrate the range of adaptations, both behavioural and metabolic, that enable many "cold-blooded" species to survive freezing temperatures. Bullfrogs and leopard frogs move into deeper water. Their responses to cold are different from those of the wood frogs and spring peepers that overwinter on land about the woodland marsh. The river amphibians are not able to survive even brief periods of freezing, and must avoid such temperatures. They do this by burrowing into the unfrozen mud on the river bottom. When buried, their metabolic and heart rate decrease, brain activity slows and breathing stops. The intake of water and exchange of oxygen and carbon dioxide occur through the skin. These amphibians remain in this state of hibernation until the water warms again.

The wood frogs and spring peepers spend the winter near the surface of the ground. They actually freeze, but in a way that enables them to thaw and recover when it warms in spring. These species burrow into a thick layer of leaves or overwinter within the protection of a tangle of tree roots covered by leaves and rotting wood. The snow provides additional insulation in both sites. Researchers have shown that the temperatures in their hibernation sites fall to only -5° to -7° C, although the air temperatures may be much colder. This range is critical, for they are unable to survive temperatures that are only a few degrees lower.

Internally, wood frogs and spring peepers limit freezing to the water that is outside the cells, and they control the formation of ice so that their tissues are not damaged. In doing this, however, they must also keep the water inside the cells from freezing, for the cells continue to function, although at a much reduced rate, through the period of hibernation.

In autumn, these amphibians produce two types of proteins that accumulate in the fluids around the cells. One seeds the formation of small ice crystals, and the second combines with these small crystals and prevents them from coalescing into large crystals. Thus, the fluid outside the cells freezes, but in the form of small crystals that do not damage the tissues.

Also in autumn, these frogs store large amounts of carbohydrates and, stimulated by the onset of freezing temperatures, convert them into simple sugars. Sugars such as glucose accumulate inside the cells and lower the temperature at which the cell fluids freeze. Many other animals use glycerol in a similar fashion, not unlike our practice of adding antifreeze to car radiators to lower the freezing point of the coolant.

The cells maintain a low level of metabolic activity while surrounded by ice. Oxygen and other substances usually carried by the blood are not available because breathing has stopped and the blood is frozen. Nevertheless, the cells generate energy by fermenting the sugars that accumulated within them before freezing.

In ways such as these, some frogs and a variety of other animals are able to survive freezing temperatures, provided they have well-insulated hibernacula for protection from extreme cold. With the warmth of spring, the ice crystals melt, the blood thaws and the heart begins to beat. Gradually, the frog revives and joins the evening choruses that proclaim another spring.

Needed Habitats

The habitat must provide for the metabolic needs of its inhabitants, even when they are in a state of dormancy. A healthy river system provides all requirements for survival, during both summer and winter. Polluted water and damaged river banks reduce the chances of survival, especially in winter. Clean water and intact river banks are the year-round responsibilities of the adjacent communities and land owners.

A SPECIAL PLACE AND A SPECIAL BIRD

A river is a peaceful place to visit. Whether it is the history of the community, the displays of wildflowers or the activities of wild animals, a river stimulates a desire to explore and to know things. Few habitats better acquaint people with the world around them. A healthy river is a community treasure, an attraction for both local people and visitors.

Sweet Rocket

The Habitant River curves away from the southeast corner of the property and crosses to the opposite side of the dykelands. There is a bench beside this curve that is one of our special places. From the bench we can look eastward for a kilometre or more over the dykelands and meandering river. Downstream, cattle and horses from the farm on the opposite upland are pastured on the meadows. The gentle breeze on the meadows is cool and refreshing, and there is nothing to do but enjoy the wildlife and admire the sunset. It is a pleasant place to sit on a warm summer evening

On most evenings there are ducks on the river, shorebirds among the reeds, and warblers and sparrows in the bushes. Swallows sail over the water and gracefully dip for a drink, while kingbirds splash along for theirs. Chimney swifts circle high in the sky during the late evening and, at night, owls glide down from the mountain to hunt and fish. From spring to fall, the displays of wildflowers change continuously.

River-bank Flowers

There are patches of wild raspberries and roses around the bench, and red osier grows on the lower bank. The spring colours start in May when the shadbush and wild cherry come into blossom, and continue through late June with displays of sweet rockets.

Sweet rocket, or dame's rocket, is not a native plant, but one introduced from Europe for ornamental purposes. It escaped from the gardens and now, at The Old Place, forms colourful beds along the driveway and carpets large areas of the meadow and river bank. Many plants are a metre tall and have showy clusters of flowers at the tops of their stems. Most flowers are white, but some are pink or purple, and all are highly fragrant. The individual flower is in the shape of a flared tube opening with four flat petals. These four petals, forming a cross, as well as the slender seed pods that develop later, identify sweet rocket as a member of the mustard family.

Wild morning-glory, or hedge bindweed, is a conspicuous flower in mid summer. It is a vine and trails through the grasses and over the bushes, and may reach three metres in length. Morning-glory also has an extensive root system and is an effective means of binding the soil on the bank. The tip of each branch constantly bends back and forth searching for a support to coil around. Its scientific name describes both this habit and its habitat: *Convolvulus* means "to entwine" and *sepium* refers to "hedges". The flowers grow along the length of the vine. Each is large and showy, bell-shaped, and pink with white stripes. Bees are numerous when morning-glory is in flower, and their path into each flower is a precise one. They alight at the edge of the bell and follow fine pink lines within the white stripes. These lines guide them to the centre of the flower where the nectar is stored in tiny wells.

Morning-glory

Asters, goldenrods and tansies provide the colour displays of autumn. Tansy is a tall plant with clusters of intensely yellow flowers and leaves that are divided into fern-like leaflets. The plants are strongly scented because the leaves and stems contain an oil called tanacetin or, simply, oil of tansy. Its bright flowers and strong scent are pleasant additions to a walk about the meadow in August and September. Like many flowers of the meadow, tansy is not a native plant. The early settlers brought it here and it has spread widely since then. The settlers used the plant for medicinal purposes, and they extracted a bright yellow dye from its crushed flowers and leaves for use when making clothing. Tansy, either fresh or dried, is also a good insect repellent and was placed in clothes closets for that purpose.

When we are sitting on the bench in the evening, it is not unusual to see a fox running along the river bank or following the fences that cross the meadows. Foxes usually hunt at night and

Foxes

may travel several kilometres or more from their dens. The red fox is the only species that lives here, but several colour phases occur. Cross foxes have a dark patch or cross between the shoulders, silver foxes are black with white-tipped hairs, and black foxes are all black. All colour phases belong to the same species and may occur in the same litter. The red phase is the one usually seen, dark foxes are now very rare. The black phase must have been more numerous 300 years ago, for records written in the time of Champlain list it as one of the animals hunted for its fur by the Mi'kmaq people.

Red Fox

One June a few years ago, we found a family of foxes while birding along the foot of the mountain. Their den was under a tangle of tree roots near a recently cleared field. It was late afternoon and the adults were outside the den with their four young. Young foxes play like puppies, wrestling and tumbling over one another, and we watched them for half an hour. The young remain with their parents until autumn, when they leave to establish their own home territories.

A Special Bird

Sometimes on summer evenings we go to the bench just to watch the chimney swifts. The swifts disperse far and wide during the day to search for flying insects, but in the evening they gather over the dykelands before going to a communal roost. A few swifts arrive first, but soon thirty or forty birds are circling with rapid wing beats. The swifts are special.

There is a chimney in a neighbouring town where swifts roost each evening. They come from all directions at dusk, circle erratically for several minutes and then start to enter the chimney, at first a few at a time and then almost all of them in a descending funnel. Some nights we count up to 900 swifts at this roost. The town residents have become fascinated by them and stroll down to the chimney at dusk, first to listen for the chittering calls and to point out the early arrivals, then to watch the swifts collect and try to count them, and finally to applaud after the swifts funnel into the chimney. It has become a nightly ritual.

Chimney Swift

A few years ago, the Town Council decided to remove the old building but, working with the Blomidon Naturalists Society, a local group, demolition proceeded in a way that protected the chimney for the swifts. When the swifts returned the following spring, their chimney was a centrepiece for a nature display and a miniature park. Local residents and visitors continue to stroll downtown each evening to await the arrival of the swifts and to enjoy the sunset.

This was not the only time that local naturalists acted to save the chimney swifts. In 1974 the swifts returned as usual in early May, but in late May the weather turned colder and there were several days of freezing rain and snow. On May 26, it practically "rained" swifts as birds collapsed from starvation and exhaustion in mid flight and dropped to the ground. We picked up about 900 swifts from the wet grass, from puddles on the sidewalks, from between vehicles on the streets, and we ran about catching swifts as they fell like we caught baseballs when we were in school. Most were dead or died shortly thereafter. We placed the others in open, low-temperature incubators to warm and dry, and then the task of feeding them began.

Strained liver and a little glucose and water were given to each bird, and by the time they were all fed it was time to start again. The local radio station announced regular reports and a number of people came to help. They were organized into teams and took turns feeding the swifts. The feeding schedule took twenty-four hours each day and continued through the four days of the storm. On a warm and sunny fifth day, about 200 swifts were taken to a nearby pond and released, and the tired rescuers enjoyed the reward of watching the birds again swooping over the water and catching insects.

The chimney swift story is an excellent example of local nature stewardship. These birds would have had no roost had the chimney been demolished, and all certainly would have died had they been left in the cold, wet grass or on the street. Now as we watch the swifts wheeling over the dykelands, we wonder how many of them are descended from the birds that the community and local naturalists rescued on those two occasions.

Nature Centre

Local Nature Stewardship

THE MEADOW GARDEN

"Here in this tender acre beside the tide…"
The Little Field of Peace
Charles G.D. Roberts, 1896

A TIDAL MARSH AND A MEADOW

Many regions of the world require continuous irrigation to grow crops, and this irrigation adds salts to the soil. Tidal-marsh plants are remarkable in that they can conserve water, regulate internal salt levels and produce a high yield. We will need to know more about these plants if we are to develop crop plants for areas where salt accumulation and lack of water limit the production of food.

Tidal Marsh

Three hundred years ago, the meadow at The Old Place was part of the Habitant Creek tidal marsh. At first dykes were built along the river channel to control flooding by the rising tide. Later, a dyke was constructed across the mouth of the Creek, with an aboiteau in the river bed, to stop the tide from flowing upstream. As the water and salt drained from the soil, the tidal marsh gradually changed into a meadow.

Up to eighteen cubic kilometres of water flow into the Minas Basin with each tide, fill the Basin and flood the marshes on the seaward side of the dyke. The tides peak every twelve hours and twenty-five minutes and rise to a height of fifteen metres and sometimes higher. Their churning and eroding actions add such a high content of sand and clay particles to the inshore water that it is a muddy reddish-brown in colour. As the water flows over the marshes and the current loses its force, and as the tide begins to recede, these particles settle around the vegetation in the form of a rich mud. The process began about 5000 years ago and still continues. Today, a deep layer of nutrient-rich sediment forms the meadow at The Old Place and neighbouring marshes.

We can see how quickly the tides build the local marshes simply by comparing the heights of the land on either side of the most recent dyke. In the twenty years since its construction, the marsh on the seaward side has become almost two metres higher than the adjacent field on the landward side. This build-up results from the twice-daily flooding that both deposits new sediments and maintains a high water content in those already deposited. On the landward side, the land is drained and more compacted.

Tidal marshes are rich in nutrients and so are the meadows claimed by dyking them. Compared to the adjacent upland soils, dyked fields contain a higher organic content because they were formed by sediment accumulating around plants; and they contain three to six times more potassium, magnesium, calcium and phosphorus because such minerals were concentrated by the flooding and drying that accompanied the rising and ebbing of the tide.

The European settlers recognized the richness of the dyke-lands. Settlement spread quickly along the marshes, dykes were built and extended, and the tidal marshes were claimed and used to pasture cattle and sheep. The settlers also grew peas, corn, wheat, oats and barley on the dykelands, as well as such root crops as beets and turnips, and flax for spinning and weaving. Hay quickly became a major crop, and by the mid 1800s it was marketed in centres as far away as Boston. The early dykeland farmers planted "English hay", a mixture of red and white clovers, with timothy, red-top and couch grasses.

Because of its high nutrient content, the early farmers spread marsh mud over their upland fields as a fertilizer, a practice that continued into the 1900s. The "mud diggers" worked in winter, between tides, cutting brick-sized blocks from the sides of the river channel. The diggers worked in pairs; one cut the blocks and the other pitched them to the top of the bank with a fork. The farmers hauled these blocks away with horses and sleds and ploughed them into their fields in spring.

The early farmers also harvested grass from the upper marsh, cutting it between tides and stacking it on posts or staddles above the water to dry. Alternatively, they simply tied the hay into bales or placed it on rafts and allowed it to float to shore on the incoming tide. It was used in winter as "salt hay" fodder. The horses were fitted with "mud shoes" when working on the marshes, wide metal plates strapped to their hooves, to keep them from sinking into the mud.

A tidal marsh, like any ecosystem, has many unique features. Its plants are adapted to a high salt environment that alternately floods and dries and they are different from those that live

Staddle

A Unique Ecosystem

Salt-marsh Cordgrass

on the uplands. Exploring the marsh below the dyke helps explain how plants live in this harsh environment, and how they helped build the meadow at The Old Place.

Salt concentrations of only a few parts per million would kill the plants that grow on the adjacent uplands. Upland plants, like corn, die when placed in sea water because water moves from a fluid of low salt concentration into one of high salt content. Thus, water within the low-salt tissues of the corn passes out into the high-salt seawater, and the plant dies from dehydration although it is surrounded by water.

Tidal-marsh plants, unlike upland plants, are flooded by water that contains about 3% salt, and some plants require high salt levels to stimulate growth. While tidal-marsh plants can obtain water from their surroundings, the challenge is to control their internal salt levels. On the one hand, they must accumulate a higher level of salt than is present in the seawater in order to draw in water from the sea. On the other hand, too much salt inhibits the plant's metabolism and stops growth. Tidal-marsh plants control their internal levels of salt in several ways. Some plants are designed to control the amount of salt that enters, others store salt but in a way that does not harm the plant, and many are able to excrete excess salt.

The process of photosynthesis used by some tidal-marsh plants also differs from that used by many upland species. While the process requires more energy, it uses carbon dioxide and water more efficiently. Conservation of water is important to plants that grow in a high salt environment. By controlling salt levels and conserving water, tidal-marsh plants are able to maintain high productivity although regularly flooded by the tide.

Tidal-marsh Grasses

Salt-marsh and salt-meadow cordgrasses are the most numerous plants on the seaward side of the dyke. Both are wonderfully adapted to live on the tidal marsh. We find salt-marsh cordgrass on the outer marsh where it forms a dense carpet along the river channel and is flooded by the tide. These plants have coarse stems and long, tapered leaves, and measure up to a metre in height. Salt-meadow cordgrass is not as tall and has finer stems that often bend in a swirled pattern. We look for it on the inner marsh where it is flooded for shorter periods during high tides. The salt-meadow cordgrasses mature in autumn and their flower-heads collectively cast a purplish haze over the inner marsh.

Both cordgrasses belong to the group of plants that can photosynthesize while submerged, and they are able to control their salt content both by limiting intake and excreting excess amounts. They have a layer of cells in their roots, as do many tidal-marsh plants, that are specially designed to control the intake of water and salt. The cordgrasses also have numerous salt-excreting glands embedded in the surfaces of their leaves. Under a microscope, each gland looks like a tiny hair and each hair acts as a microscopic bladder. That is, the "hair" accumulates salt, swells and ruptures to release the salt that is then washed away by the tide.

The cordgrasses play an important role in aerating marsh soils. The soils are heavy, water-logged clays that are deficient in oxygen. Internally, the cordgrasses have ducts that pass from the leaves down the stems to the smallest roots. These pathways conduct air into the substrate, enhancing plant growth and enabling small animals to dig and burrow into the mud.

Both cordgrasses help build and maintain the tidal marsh. As sediment settles from the water and gradually accumulates, they produce new roots that bind it in place and, as the soil deepens, the lower roots decompose and add organic matter to the soil. Especially in winter when the drifting ice has sheared off the upper parts of the plants, the roots and stubble help stabilize the marsh. Today, these cordgrasses do not grow at The Old Place, but we only need to dig down about thirty centimetres to find a layer of peat formed from them years ago.

The cordgrasses also contribute to the estuarine and marine systems well beyond the borders of the tidal marsh. They produce large amounts of organic material that is washed into the estuary where it is broken down by the action of enormous populations of bacteria. A number of invertebrate animals feed on this detritus, or directly on the bacteria. In turn, fish, birds and other vertebrates feast on these invertebrates.

American beach-grass is another plant that once helped build the meadow at The Old Place. Beach-grass grows in the sand

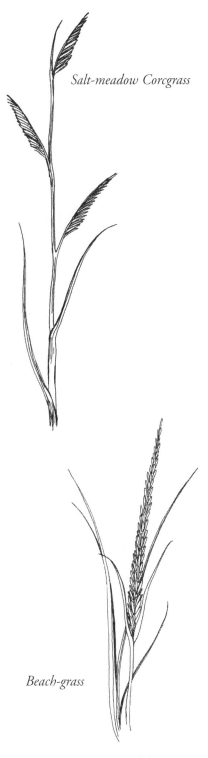

Salt-meadow Corcgrass

Beach-grass

above the usual high tide levels. Its scientific name is an appropriate one, for *Amnophila* means "a lover of sand", and sand actually stimulates the plant's growth. That is, in response to the accumulation of sand, beach-grass produces new roots and leaves that bind the sand in place, and root systems of several metres in length may be formed. This is why beach-grass is often planted to stabilize sandy beaches and dunes. On the other hand, removal of the sand stops plant growth. Footpaths and careless use of vehicles may expose the roots, stop growth, and allow the wind and water a chance to start eroding the marsh.

Beach-grass must also conserve water and protect itself against salt sprays. Two ways in which it does this may be seen by examining a leaf with a hand-lens. The lower surface is a thick, protective layer. The upper surface has grooves that run the length of the leaf and gases are exchanged through pores in these grooves. In dry weather, the leaves curl tightly around the stem, closing the pores and conserving moisture, and the protective layer is exposed to the salt sprays.

Tidal-marsh Flowers

Samphire

We always look for samphire or slender glasswort when exploring the tidal marsh. It is a flowering plant. Like all seashore plants, it requires water and shows several modifications in structure that are designed to retain a supply of it. Samphire has thick, fleshy branches and stems in which large amounts of water are stored. On the other hand, to minimize the loss of water through evaporation, its leaves are small and scale-like. Ducks and other animals eat samphire for water, and people slice the young plants into salads for their moist, crisp texture. Some samphires turn red in late summer, and the colours of the autumn marsh are often the greens and reds of samphires mixed with the browns and yellows of the cordgrasses.

Samphire, more so than many marsh plants, can grow in sites of especially high salinity and is often the pioneer plant that settles in areas where the marsh has been damaged. Patches of marsh surface may be stripped of all vegetation by ice or human activity. Deprived of plant shelter, the surface bakes in the sun, water evaporates and salt is concentrated. These high salt levels kill most plants and inhibit the germination of seeds. However, samphires are able to grow in these sites and gradually provide the shade needed to reduce evaporation and salinity. Other marsh plants are then able to spread into the area. It requires three or four years for the cordgrasses to become re-established and the marsh surface restored.

Goosefoot, or orach, and sea-rocket are two other plants that we find on the upper parts of the tidal marsh. Goosefoot is a large, spreading plant and is so-named because its leaves are lobed and triangular, resembling in outline the print of a goose's foot. The leaves are thick and store water, and their surfaces appear gray and powdery because they are covered with numerous, hair-like salt glands. These glands excrete excess salt as do those described for the cordgrasses.

Sea-rocket, or sea mustard, is a large, bushy plant. It also has thick leaves and stems, designed to store water. Sea-rocket flowers from July to September. The flowers are pink and, like all mustards, have four petals that form a cross. Its seed capsules resemble a rocket. These capsules have thick shells and survive in salt water until they are deposited high on the beach by spring tides. The seeds germinate on relatively dry land after a period of especially high tides.

These are some of the plants that once grew at The Old Place and helped build the meadow. With the construction of the dykes, they were replaced by cultivated grasses and the tidal marsh was changed into a hayfield. However, the dyke broke in 1944 and salt water flowed over the fields with each tide. The water carried marsh plants and seeds and the cordgrasses again grew at The Old Place. Three years after a new dyke was built and the meadow reclaimed, patches of marsh plants continued to grow in the hay, often in depressions where salt presumably had accumulated. Not surprisingly, goosefoot and sea-rocket were the most persistent, for they are the best able to survive a wide range of salinities and dehydration.

Tidal-marsh plants grow in a high-salt environment, they conserve water and produce a high yield. Today, increasingly, we must grow crops under conditions of water shortages and rising

Goosefoot

Sea-rocket

Needed Information

85

salt levels. Tidal-marsh plants can help by providing the needed clues and genetic information. We must know more about these plants. Useful information on topics such as species present, abundance, habitats, plant succession and plant associations can be recorded by naturalists. Tidal-marsh ecosystems contain valuable information and must be conserved with care.

A WALK ON THE TIDAL MARSH

The European settlers started dyking and draining the marshes and the practice still continues. These settlers did not know about the life and dynamics of a tidal marsh. Today we can measure its high productivity and calculate its contribution to the adjacent estuarine and marine systems. We are learning about the diverse forms of plant and animal life that are so wonderfully adapted to live in such an environment, we know that it is an important nursery and feeding area for coastal fish, that it is important to agriculturalists developing crops with salt tolerance, and we are beginning to understand the importance of a marsh as a pollutant-removing filter between terrestrial and marine systems. We now know that these remarkable environments must be protected, that they can no longer be destroyed by dyking and draining or by any other means.

While cordgrasses are the dominant plants on the tidal marsh, other plants and a variety of animals live among them and also cope successfully with the harsh environment. We visit the marsh regularly through the seasons to look for these plants and animals, for they too lived at The Old Place in the days before the dykes were built.

Tidal-marsh Plants

Several sedges and rushes grow on the tidal marsh. It takes practice to distinguish these two groups from one another and from grasses. The stems of grasses are hollow and jointed. Sedges have stems that lack joints, are usually solid and often are triangular in cross-section ("sedges have edges"). The stems of rushes also lack joints, but those of most rushes are round and hollow and not triangular and solid.

Seashore spike-grass, marsh sedge and black grass are examples of the grasses, sedges and rushes that are common on the tidal marsh. Black grass is a rush and not a true grass. We find borders of it along the inner part of the marsh, where the large clumps look brownish from a distance. Its stems are tall and erect, and its flower clusters are near the tops of long stalks. Black grass has a simple way of getting rid of excess salt, a method used by many tidal-marsh plants. The extra salt is stored in its grass-like leaves and is eliminated when the leaves die and fall off.

Black Grass

Marsh Plants

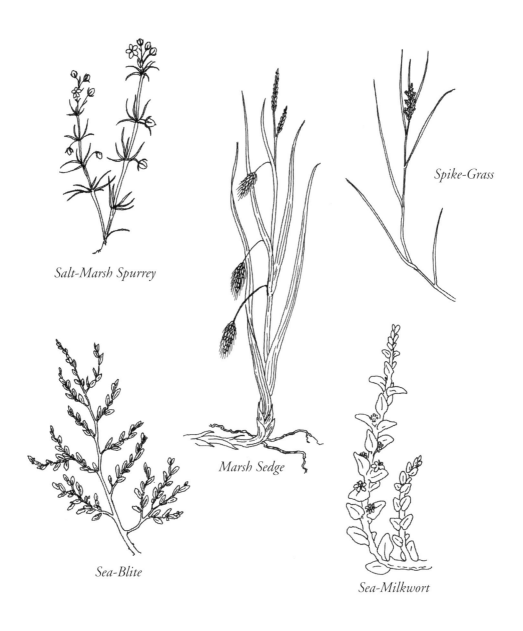

Salt-Marsh Spurrey

Spike-Grass

Marsh Sedge

Sea-Blite

Sea-Milkwort

Black grass grows from long underground stems, called rhizomes, and each stem gives rise to a number of plants along its length. Extensive networks of roots also grow from the stems and penetrate deeply into the soil, and firmly bind it in place. Black grass grows and regenerates quickly, and was the plant that the early dyke builders preferred when sodding the surface of a new dyke.

There are several plants that we look for in mid summer. They produce striking displays of flowers. Salt-marsh spurrey is a type of carnation and has showy pink flowers. Sea-milkwort of the primrose family also has pink flowers, although they are smaller than the blossoms of other primroses. Sea-blite is a sprawling plant with tiny, green flowers clustered in the axils of its leaves. The leaves of these plants are fleshy and store water. They also store excess salt in special pockets where it is diluted by the stored water.

Sea lavender flowers in late summer. Each flower is small, but many of them edge its branches with a hazy blue colour. New plants grow from the base of the stem and form attractive clusters of lavender. The leaves are thick and filled with tiny pockets that store salt and water, and they have salt glands to excrete excess salt. Its long root grows straight down to reach the less saline water in the deeper levels of the soil. Lavender is often collected and dried for use in flower arrangements. Unfortunately, it is also collected in large quantities for commercial purposes, a practice that may threaten the future of this beautiful plant. It should be cultivated for commercial use and the wild plants left for everyone to enjoy.

Sea Lavender

Tidal-marsh Animals

Many animals live on the tidal marsh, and a search for them illustrates both the variety of animal types and the curious ways in which they cope with high salt levels, with drying and heating in the sun at low tide and with submersion at high tide. Animals with gills must retain a supply of oxygen for use when the tide is low, and those with lungs need oxygen for use when submerged at high tide.

Cordgrass forms a dense matting over the marsh that helps maintain humidity and temperature levels at the soil surface during low tide. Enormous numbers of animals live within the shelter of this canopy. Snails forage on algae, insects and spiders live and reproduce on stems and leaves, and crabs scurry about on the damp mud. Fish swarm over the marsh at high tide to feed on these and other invertebrates, and ducks and other marsh birds feast on them at low water. The tracks of raccoons and mink record their visits to catch crabs and fish stranded at low tide.

Tidal-marsh Invertebrates

Mud Snail

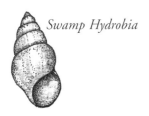

Swamp Hydrobia

Salt-marsh Snail

Green Sea-slug

Three types of snails are common on the tidal marsh: the mud snail, swamp hydrobia and salt-marsh snail. The shell of the mud snail, or mud dog whelk, is dark brown and has a tall spire. It is the largest of the three species, about two centimetres long. Dense aggregations of mud snails crawl along the stream banks feeding on the algae that coat the mud. Mud snails simply burrow into the moist mud to prevent drying when the tide is low. Swamp hydrobia is the smallest of the three, only a half centimetre or less in size. Its shell is yellowish and glassy and has swollen whorls. As the tide lowers, hydrobia fills its shell with water, closes the opening and remains bathed in the water until the tide rises. The salt-marsh snail has a brown or creamy shell with dark-brown bands. It is an air-breather, unlike the previous two which have gills, and climbs up and down the stalks of grass to stay above the water. However, it needs to take air into its shell only once every one or two hours and, if submerged briefly at high tide, this allows sufficient time for it to wait for the water to lower.

Another mollusc we look for is the green sea-slug, or emerald sea-slug. It is a small slug, one or two centimetres long, that is bright green when well fed. Unlike most molluscs it lacks a shell. Green sea-slugs live in the mats of algae found in ditches and pools, but they are hard to find and our searches are often unsuccessful. The green sea-slug feeds on algae and incorporates the algal chloroplasts into its own cells. These chloroplasts give the slug its green colour. The chloroplasts remain functional in light and generate sugars and oxygen by photosynthesis in the same way as they did in the algae. For this reason, green sea-slugs are sometimes referred to as "plants that crawl".

Insects are numerous on the tidal marsh, particularly horse flies, deer flies, mosquitoes, and a great variety of beetles. Some insects swim or float, buoyed up by surface tension, when the tide is high; and others retreat into air pockets in plants or the substrate to survive the period of submergence.

Horse flies, like all flies, have just one pair of wings. Some species have bright green eyes and are called greenheads. The larvae of these flies are aquatic and survive the period until the tide rises in water-filled depressions or by burrowing into the moist mud. The emergence of adult flies from the pupal stage is synchronized with the tides. They emerge as soon as the water level starts to drop. This provides the maximum time for their exoskeletons to harden and enables them to fly off before the water again floods the marsh.

Horse flies feed on nectar and plant juices. In addition, the females require blood protein for egg production and can inflict sharp bites on naturalists exploring the marsh. Their mouth parts are designed not simply to pierce the skin, but to cut so that a pool of blood collects. The males are strictly vegetarians.

Salt-marsh greenheads are common on the inner marsh where they live about salt-meadow cordgrass. Other species live in association with different plant types. When we visit the marsh in early morning in summer, we often see a swarm of salt-marsh greenheads hovering just above the cordgrass. These are male greenheads and they begin hovering as the temperatures warm following sunrise. Researchers believe that hovering and swarming are premating behaviours, both common to many insects that mate while in flight. Salt-marsh greenheads hover near a site, such as a water-filled ditch, where the females that emerged during the night will take flight. As the females fly, the males make rapid pursuit flights to capture them. While hovering increases the chances of finding a mate, the large concentration of insects also attracts many hungry swallows and dragonflies.

Greenhead

Spiders are numerous on the marsh, where they live on mats of algae and on the stems and leaves of cordgrass. There are many species, but we have identified only a few. Some types, like the long-jawed spiders, construct cobwebs to catch the insects on which they feed, and their cobwebs coated with dew decorate the marsh in early morning. Other species, like wolf spiders, do not make webs, but are adapted in other ways to capture prey. They have especially acute eyesight that can detect even slight motions,

Wolf Spider

their legs are sensitive to vibrations such as may be caused by insect movements, they are fast and some can even jump. Although spiders are terrestrial animals, they are able to survive submergence for up to a few hours when the tide is high.

We frequently see the shells of rock and green crabs during a walk on the tidal marsh. These crabs live under the cordgrass canopy and among the layers of seaweed that accumulate along streams and in tide-pools. Their shells are shed and replaced periodically to allow the animals to grow in size, and most of the empty shells seen on the marsh are the result of this moulting. Crabs scurry about scavenging on worms and small invertebrates, and on dead fish and other carrion. In turn, crabs are eaten by many animals such as flounders, gulls, great blue herons, raccoons and mink.

When the tide is low, crabs simply find a water-filled depression in the mud, or scoop one out, and remain in it until the water rises again. They do not have the problem with internal salt levels experienced by many marsh animals because they can tolerate a wide range of salinities, and their internal salt levels are usually the same as those of the surrounding water. Their kidneys eliminate especially high levels of salt. Crabs respond to the temperature changes that accompany the rising and ebbing of the tide by varying their metabolic rate. That is, when the temperature drops, they generate heat by increasing their metabolism, and they lower their metabolism when temperatures rise. At very low temperatures, crabs burrow into the mud, reduce their metabolism to a state of dormancy, and remain inactive until the environment becomes warmer. They also burrow into the moist mud to avoid excess heat, but it is not uncommon to find dead crabs that were apparently stranded by the lowering tide and killed by high temperatures and drying.

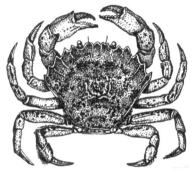

Green Crab

Tidal-marsh Fish

Tidal marshes are crucial to the well being of estuarine and coastal fish. Like a nursery they provide young fish with an abundance of food, and schools of adult fish, both local and those migrating along the coast, swarm over the marshes with the flooding tide to feed. They feed on the enormous numbers of insects, crustaceans and other invertebrates. About forty-five species of fish occur on local tidal marshes. Predators, such as dogfish, small thresher and mackerel (porbeagle) sharks, chase these schools of fish; and ducks, like red-breasted mergansers, dive to feed on the smaller ones. Most fish withdraw as the water lowers and a few hours later they may be five or six kilometres away waiting for the next high tide to return to the marsh.

Not all fish move back and forth with the tide. We find many small fish, such as mummichogs, sticklebacks, silversides and smelt, in pools and wet ditches when the water lowers. Mummichogs can tolerate the wide ranges of salinity, temperature and oxygen that occur in the tidal marshes. This allows them to survive in stagnant pools or to swim through the aboiteaux and travel short distances upstream into fresh water. On the marsh, mummichogs may move in and out with the tide, or they may burrow into the moist mud during low tide and emerge again when the water rises. Some even overwinter in the mud.

Mummichog

We see many birds on the tidal marsh, although the variety is not large. Herons and other shorebirds forage along the creeks and pools; black ducks are common, as are herring, black-backed and ring-billed gulls; crows are plentiful; and an occasional bald eagle sails over the marsh looking for food. These birds feed on the huge populations of marsh insects and other invertebrates, and on the fish and marine organisms stranded by the falling tide.

Like many plants and animals of the tidal marsh, birds must also be able to eliminate the excess salt taken in with food and water. Many marsh birds have special glands for this purpose, as do marine species. These salt or nasal glands specifically remove salt from the blood and excrete it by way of the nostrils. Salt glands are highly efficient, and some species can eliminate salt within a few minutes and others within one or two hours of ingestion. Marine birds have well-developed salt glands, but the size of those of tidal-marsh species is related to the amount of time spent on the marsh. That is, individuals that live inland have poorly developed salt glands, whereas individuals of the same species that frequent the tidal marsh have well-developed glands.

We always look for sharp-tailed sparrows when visiting the tidal marsh. They have ochre-coloured facial markings and gray

Tidal-Marsh Birds

Sharp-tailed Sparrow

ear patches. Sharp-tails live on the upper marsh, but it is a challenge to find them for they usually remain on the ground among the grasses, where they feed on the numerous insects and abundant beach-hoppers, a type of crustacean. However, the extended "buss"-like calls uttered during their short flights signal their presence.

Nesting is a precarious task for birds that live on the marsh. Sharp-tailed sparrows build their nest in a hummock of grass several centimetres above ground. Although the upper marsh is not flooded by the usual daily tides, it may be by the higher tides that occur in cycles of about twenty-six days. Allowing a few days to construct a nest and lay eggs, ten days for incubation and another ten days until the young fledge, these birds can just raise their brood during the period between these higher tides. There is little room for error.

Not all tidal-marsh birds nest on the marsh. The willet usually nests on the adjacent hayfields and uplands, but within commuting distance for it feeds and loafs on the tidal marsh. The young are led to the marsh by their parents within hours of hatching. They remain on the marsh, scampering back and forth with the tide, for almost a month before they start to fly. Occasionally, willets do nest on the upper marsh, above the usual high-tide levels. However, the prolonged nesting period, eight to ten days to lay a clutch of eggs and three weeks for incubation, makes them vulnerable to very high tides and especially so when winds and stormy seas accompany the tide.

Willet

Tidal-marsh Mammals

White-sided Dolphin

We regularly see harbour seals and porpoises swimming up to the dyke, and sometimes a pod of white-sided dolphins. They are chasing schools of fish. The dolphins occasionally become stranded in the stream beds that cross the marsh. Presumably, being deep-sea mammals, they are unaccustomed to the gently sloping shore and the rapidly falling tide. July 31, 1991 was such an occasion. In late evening four white-sided dolphins were stranded in a river bed on the upper marsh. They refloated when the tide rose the following morning and were escorted out to sea.

Marine mammals likely continued upriver to the present site of The Old Place in the days before the dykes were built.

Perhaps porpoises once circled the marsh where the riding ring is now, and seals once hauled up the bank and dozed in the sun on the lawn — not unlike the incumbent.

Tidal marshes support enormous numbers of plants and animals, and are crucial to the well-being of the adjacent estuarine and marine systems. Nevertheless, tidal marshes are rapidly becoming endangered places for they continue to be destroyed as communities and industries expand. About 75% of those in Atlantic Canada have been lost. A failure to recognize their value is the primary reason. Communities and land owners must make a special effort to protect these endangered habitats.

Endangered Places

THE MEADOW PATH

No one knows how many plants and animals live on earth for the diversity is immense. We do know that the present rate of habitat loss and degradation, through physical destruction and chemical contamination, means that many populations are now in decline and that species are becoming extinct at an accelerating rate. We know that we are losing the biological information needed to develop new foods, medicines and natural systems that purify air and water. We are also losing the challenges and pleasures of knowing about living things. Communities and land owners can help conserve the diversity of life by setting land aside and allowing it to remain wild.

The meadow path follows the river bank and then curves westward across the field to a wooded area. Several plants are conspicuous along the path and a variety of small animals live with them, some in association with specific plants.

Flowers and Insects

Clusters of wild irises, or blue flags, grow beside the path in moist areas of the meadow. They bloom between mid June and early July, at the same time as the bobolinks are nesting. While our irises are blue, wild irises found elsewhere in the world are of various colours as are the garden varieties. The word "iris" comes from a Greek word that means "rainbow", and describes the range of colours shown by the different varieties. The iris is the "fleur-de-lis", the heraldic ensign of French royalty. Louis VII was the king who first chose the iris for his ensign. His iris was a gold one.

The blue sepals have fine yellow lines leading to the centre of the flower. These are guide lines, like those described for morning-glory. That is, the bee crawls along these lines to reach the nectar, and pollination occurs when pollen carried from the last flower visited is brushed onto the pistil. Additional pollen then sticks to the bee as it crawls past the stamens and is carried away to fertilize the next flower.

Clumps of evening primrose are also scattered along the meadow path, and we see the rosettes of their thick leaves flat-

Blue Flag

tened against the ground whenever the meadow is free of snow. The new stalks grow in late spring and flowers are present from late July through September. The flowers are yellow and showy and clustered near the ends of the tall stalks. They open during late afternoon and evening, and each blossom usually lasts for only one day. Evening primroses are often more in evidence in late summer for, with the shorter days, the blossoms remain open for a longer time.

Primrose flowers are highly fragrant, particularly when ready for pollination. The scent is produced in peak amounts at dusk. This fragrance plus the bright yellow flower attracts night-flying moths, bees and other insects. Once they alight on the flower, the insects follow nectar guides to the centre of the blossom. These nectar guides, unlike those of the iris, cannot be seen by the human eye for they are formed of pigments that reflect ultraviolet light. However, the night-flying insects can detect and follow these ultraviolet paths, and pollinate the flower as they crawl toward the nectar wells.

Evening Primrose

On a walk one evening about five years ago, we noticed a beautiful yellow and pink moth on a primrose flower. Its folded wings were about one-and-a-half centimetres long and its colours perfectly matched the flower. It was a primrose moth, one of the "flower moths". Primrose moths visit the flowers at night and feed on the nectar. They also lay eggs on the flower, and the larvae eat both flowers and seeds. It is a beautiful moth and, now that we know about it, we always look for it on late evening walks.

A species of solitary bee also visits the flowers of evening primrose, usually in the early morning before the flowers begin to wilt. Many solitary bees, so-called because they live alone and not in colonies, have special adaptations designed to collect nectar and pollen from specific flowers. The pollen grains of evening primrose are joined by threads that make them difficult for many insects to collect, but the primrose bee has long bristles on its legs for this purpose. That is, the pollen rubs onto the bee when it inserts its long tongue into the flower-tube; and later, when grooming, the pollen is picked up by the bristles. The bee tunnels into the ground to construct its nest. The tunnel is branched and each branch ends in an enlarged chamber. The pollen and nectar

Primrose Moth

are packed into this chamber and form the substrate on which the bee lays an egg.

Aphid Farms

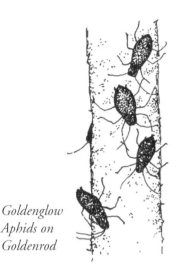

Goldenglow Aphids on Goldenrod

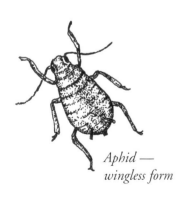

Aphid — wingless form

A variety of aphids or plant lice lives on the flowers and trees of the meadow, and many species are able to reproduce on only one type of plant. Small green aphids live on sow thistles; both red and green varieties of rose aphids live on the new growth of wild roses; brick-red goldenglow aphids live on the stems and leaves of goldenrod; small, black myzus aphids form heavy infestations on the young stems and leaves of cherries; bronze and black spruce aphids form colonies on the bark of spruce trees; and colonies of white, woolly balsam aphids appear like snow coating the new growth of fir trees.

The aphids appear in spring as the new plant growth develops. They hatch from eggs that overwintered on the bark or on the ground where the plant died back the previous fall. These first aphids are all females and lack wings. They give birth, asexually, to several generations of living young that also grow into wingless females. Large colonies of aphids are produced in this way and often infest the entire new growth of the plant. In early summer, winged females appear within the colonies. These females disperse to other plants and establish new colonies of both winged and wingless forms. These new colonies may be established on different plant species, and we have found goldenglow aphids on asters, hawkweed and ragwort as well as on goldenrod. While these colonies flourish during the summer, the aphids return to their specific host plant before laying eggs. All of these aphids are females. The males do not appear until the latter half of summer, and then the fertilized eggs are produced to overwinter and give rise to new females the following spring.

While aphids suck juices from the plants and may cause severe deformations to new growth, their associations with other insects are interesting to watch. Aphids digest the nutrients from plant juices and excrete the remainder in the form of a sweetened "honeydew", to which several species of insects are attracted. Ants are usually present at aphid colonies, and following a trail of ants that crosses the path is one way of locating aphids. The association benefits both species. Ants consume the honeydew and aphids attended by ants produce increased amounts of the syrup for them. In return, the ants protect the aphids from predators. Some insects, such as syrphid flies and ladybug beetles, lay their eggs near aphid colonies and the larvae feed on the aphids. When a syrphid fly circles the colony, the ants stand on their hind legs and wave their front legs to prevent the fly from landing and depositing its eggs. In late summer, the ants collect the fertilized aphid eggs and take them to their nests for protection over winter. In spring, they carry the eggs to nearby host plants and establish new aphid colonies and, from time to time, they transfer aphids from one plant to others to begin additional colonies.

Aphid — winged form

Meadow Butterflies

On walks in early June, we sometimes see a viceroy butterfly gliding and sailing from flower to flower. Later, on warm, sunny days when there are large patches of wild mustard blossoms, there may be a few dozen cabbage white butterflies dancing about and spiraling up into the air, and beginning in early July when the vetch starts to flower, sulphurs flit about its blue flowers.

The viceroy is a fairly large butterfly with a wing- span of up to six centimetres. Its wings are orange with black markings. Viceroys lay their eggs in late summer on willow and poplar leaves, the chief foods of their larvae. The larvae overwinter inside a rolled-up leaf. The attachment of these leaves to the twig is reinforced with strands of white silk and, unlike the other leaves, they do not drop off in autumn.

The mimic butterfly is another name for the viceroy because its colours and markings are similar to those of the much larger monarch butterfly. This is a type of protective mimicry. The monarch feeds on milkweed and obtains chemicals that are highly distasteful. While the viceroy does not have these chemicals, potential predators mistake it for a monarch and avoid eating it.

Viceroy Butterfly

A Drop of Water

There is a low area on the inner part of the meadow where water collects from spring rains, and some pools persist through much of summer. By mid June, on sunny days, we see clouds of tiny golden creatures drifting about in the water. Under a microscope these specks are seen to be water-fleas or *Daphnia*. *Daphnia* is a type of crustacean, not unlike a very small shrimp, and there

Life in a Drop of Water

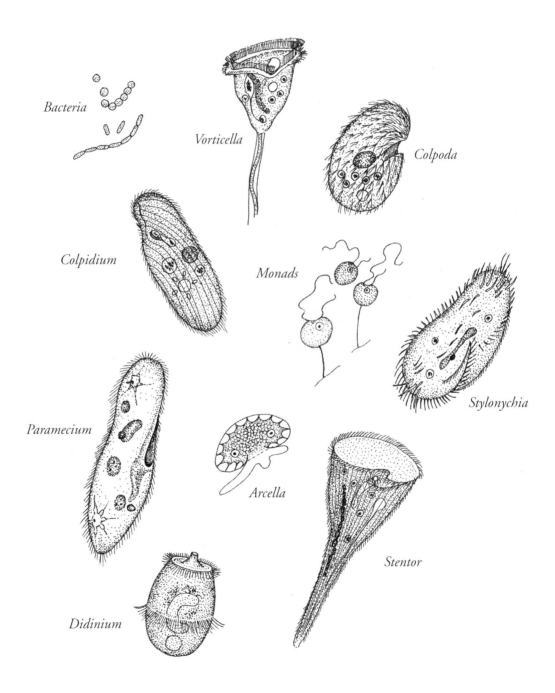

Bacteria

Vorticella

Colpoda

Colpidium

Monads

Stylonychia

Paramecium

Arcella

Stentor

Didinium

are countless numbers of them. They are able to survive in temporary pools because they produce two types of eggs. During much of the summer, they produce thin-shelled eggs that develop and hatch immediately. However, in late summer as the pool dries and temperatures drop, *Daphnia* produces a set of "winter eggs" that are enclosed by thick capsules for protection. These eggs survive drying and winter conditions and, when the water returns and warms the following spring, they hatch and give rise to a new population. Actually, the thick-shelled eggs are able to survive in dried mud for several years and then hatch when the drought is over.

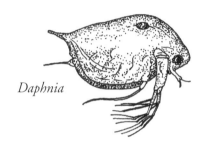

Daphnia

Daphnia is not the first organism to appear in the new pools each spring. We find a world of fascinating creatures when we look at a drop of water under a microscope, and we watch an ongoing succession of different animals when we check the water over a period of several weeks. At first, when the pools fill, only chains of rod-shaped and spherical bacteria are present. However, several types of protozoans, like monads, appear within a few days and feed on the bacteria. Monads swim by lashing their long flagella back and forth. Then species such as *Colpoda, Colpidium, Paramecium* and *Stylonychnia* appear. These species have cilia, and are propelled through the water by the synchronized beating of these hair-like "oars". Because of its shape, *Paramecium* is also called the slipper animal. It swims rapidly, with a spiral motion. *Paramecium* reaches peak numbers in about two weeks, and then the voracious feeders like *Didinium* and *Aracella* appear. *Didinium* is an oval animal with two bands of long cilia encircling its body. Its mouth is at the end of a proboscis that can be extended to devour organisms like *Paramecium*. The succession continues, with protozoans like the bell-shaped *Vorticella* and the trumpet-shaped *Stentor* appearing, and each new population feeds on the previous one.

It is these microscopic organisms that support the swarming populations of *Daphnia* and other creatures that are, in turn, food for insect larvae and larger animals. These insects and larger animals are eaten by the amphibians and birds that we enjoy watching about the edges of the pools, and that would be absent were it not for the microscopic life.

Meadow Amphibians

Green Frog

Several amphibians live in the grass on the meadow. The green and leopard frogs are the ones most frequently seen, and the egg strings of the American toad are common in springtime pools. The adult toads, however, are more frequently found in the cultivated gardens about the house than on the meadow.

Sometimes on early morning walks, while it is still damp, we startle a green frog that gives a high-pitched shriek and leaps from the path into the tall grass. Appropriately, its species name is *clamitans*, which means "shouter" or "exclaimer". Many green frogs have dark brown or gray spots. The leopard frog also leaps to one side as we pass. It has dark spots with whitish borders. We usually find the eggs of leopard frogs in May. They are laid in clumps of jelly that are attached to submerged grasses and twigs in the deeper pools. The flat, floating egg-rafts of green frogs appear in late June and early July. The adult frogs feed on all types of worms, insects and spiders, and on the grasshoppers that are so plentiful on the meadow in late summer.

Meadow Voles and Shrews

Meadow Vole

Short-tailed Shrew

Meadow voles and short-tailed shrews also live on the dykeland. The meadow voles, or meadow mice, construct an extensive pattern of runways through the undergrass and line them with grass clippings. These runways are most obvious in winter under a light snow or thin coating of ice, for the voles remain active all winter. They also build nests that are hidden in hummocks of grass or buried in the mulch about clumps of bushes. Meadow voles undergo population fluctuations and reach peak numbers every three or four years. Predators are plentiful at such times, with harriers sailing over the meadows in summer and red-tailed hawks scanning from perch-trees in winter.

The short-tailed shrews are distinguished from mice and voles by their pointed snouts, short tails and very small eyes. Shrews are abundant on the meadow. They are social animals and several may share the same area. Like mice, they tunnel through the matted grass and build "resting" chambers along these tunnels. They leave their chambers to feed, usually at night. Shrews eat mainly insects and other invertebrates, and they enter the tunnels of mice which they also catch and eat. One of the shrew's salivary glands secretes a toxin similar to that found in poisonous snakes.

The toxin is sufficiently strong to kill a mouse, and to cause minor pain to people if bitten. The short-tailed shrew is a very active animal. Its heart rate of about 760 beats per minute is ten times faster than the human heart rate.

These are just a few of the plants and animals that live on the meadow. Many species live in association with others and are dependent on them for survival. A meadow, like a woodlot or seashore, is a mosaic of habitats of various sizes and types, sometimes called "patches". Irises require a moist soil and evening primroses a dry one; warblers inhabit shrubs, sparrows live in hedgerows and hawks soar over the entire meadow; mice like thick undergrass and amphibians need wet areas; primrose bees require primrose flowers and viceroy larvae need willow and poplar leaves; *Stentor* lives in puddles; and the world of the black myzus aphid revolves around the new growth of a cherry stem. Cultivating or mowing a field, like cutting a woodlot, and especially when replanted with a single species, reduces the number of patches and creates a more uniform habitat. A loss of habitat diversity is accompanied by a loss of living things.

Apart from our desire to know about the plants and animals that live around us, biodiversity underlies our quality of life. Biodiversity is the foundation of all industries based on living systems, such as agriculture. It is imperative that we conserve some fields about our communities and allow them to remain "wild".

Habitat Diversity Needed

BIRDING THE MEADOW

The birds of an uncut meadow differ from those of a woodland or seashore. Birds evolve patterns of behaviour that best enable each to survive in its particular habitat. Careful observation of birds shows how they have adapted to and become dependent on their habitat, and explains why many birds are unable to move to a different one should theirs be altered. It also shows that bird populations can respond quickly when their habitats are restored and protected.

When we moved to The Old Place, part of the meadow was used for pasture and the rest mowed for hay. Grazing and mowing encourage a uniform habitat that is not attractive to birds because it lacks shelters for escape from predators and severe weather, and there are no high perches for singing and look-outs. Also, ground-nesting birds are highly vulnerable to mowing and hay-making machines. Our first task was to make the meadow more attractive to wildlife. We wanted an area of uncut grass with scattered islands of shrubs and trees. The birds responded quickly as we made these changes and several species now nest on the meadow and others are regular visitors.

Many birds that live on meadows and fields where there are few trees sing while in flight. During these "song flights", the birds either circle high in the sky or hover on quivering wings just above the ground and sing continuously and loudly. This practice allows their songs to be heard more widely, and generally makes the birds more conspicuous when proclaiming their territories and performing courtship displays.

Snipe   We know that spring has arrived when we hear snipe winnowing in early April. Usually in the evening, but often at any time of the day or night, we hear their tremulous notes from high overhead as they perform their territorial and courtship displays. During the display flight, the male darts into the sky, flies rapidly and erratically in wide circles with his tail fanned, and dives repeatedly. The "winnowing" sound is caused by the wind rushing over the stiff, outer tail feathers and causing them to vibrate, and the quivering effect by the beating of the wings that interrupts the air flow over the tail. Perhaps it is described as "winnowing" because the sound resembles the noise made by the fly-wheel on the old-time machines used to winnow or separate chaff from grain.

Regardless of the explanation, listening to snipe winnowing is one of the pleasures of an evening walk in spring. Early each May, we take a walk just for that purpose, one of about five kilometres return, along a road that crosses farm fields and meadows. We can hear snipe all along this walk, for as we go from field to meadow we pass from the territory of one snipe into that of another. While the winnowing is clearly heard, we usually have to search before we locate the speck in the sky that produces it. That is why we prefer the snipe's former scientific name, for *Capella* is also the name of a star. Its current name, *Gallinago,* means "hen" and lacks distinctive character.

Snipe forage on the shores of the river at The Old Place and in wet areas on the meadow. They probe with their long bills into the mud for worms and insect larvae. We have counted as many as eight snipe at one time in mid September. Most leave in late September, although one or two may overwinter during years when there is little snow.

The rich and rollicking songs of male bobolinks are another sign that spring has arrived. Their songs defy description with words, although many authors have tried: "exuberant and tinkling", "joyous and bubbling", "liquid outpourings" and "rapturous melodies". It is easier simply to describe the singer in the words of George Gladdin as "a sort of hysterical music box".

We usually see the first male bobolinks during the second week in May, a few days before the females. The male in breeding plumage is strikingly marked: black, with buff and white patches. The female is buff-coloured with brown stripes, a pattern of camouflage shown by many birds that nest on the ground in grass and reeds. Bobolinks moult after nesting, in late July and early August, and the breeding colours of the male are replaced with buff and brown markings like those of the female.

The males begin singing soon after arrival. They perch on

Snipe

Bobolinks

Male Bobolink

clumps of reeds and on tops of bushes and their songs are heard across the meadow. Later, they hover just above the grass and sing continuously, at first to claim their nesting territories and then to begin their courtship displays. The male circles above the female as courtship progresses, with wing-tips quivering and tail fanned. Sometimes the female ignores the display and remains in the grass. At other times, she darts across the meadow with one or two males in close pursuit.

We have not found their nest, and not seriously looked for one since we are concerned that we might step on the eggs or young in the thick grass. However, there is no question but that they do nest in the uncut grass. They display over the meadow and give alarm calls when we walk too near, we see the adults flying with food and dropping into the grass, and in mid July young birds flit about among the stalks of grass and nearby bushes.

For many years, our weekly counts for the property showed that about ten bobolinks inhabited the meadow and adjacent fields most summers. Their numbers increased to thirty or forty birds in mid August as young fledged and migrating bobolinks began to arrive, and peaked at eighty to ninety birds for a few days during the last week of August. The bobolinks moved out quickly in September. Five or six birds were often present at the end of the first week, only an occasional one by the third week, and usually all had left by the beginning of October.

However, the counts changed several years ago. The bobolinks still returned each spring, performed their courtship displays and began nesting. But most left in mid July, and the flocks of late summer did not visit. Early departure means nesting failure. The reason was that farmers, now requiring two crops of hay each summer, started cutting their fields earlier and destroyed many bobolink nests. Now that the problem is recognized, several farmers delay mowing until the bobolinks fledge and a few fields are left uncut. The bobolinks are again nesting successfully. In early August 1996 we counted forty bobolinks on the meadow and adjacent fields, the largest number for several years. We hope that bobolinks will nest in the areas reserved for them, and that their striking colours, bubbling songs and courtship displays will remain a part of springtime at The Old Place.

Female Bobolink

Tree swallows usually arrive during the second week in April, when six or eight circle over the meadow catching insects or skimming along the river for a drink. We place four swallow houses about the meadow each spring. The one on the bank overlooking the river is occupied first for swallows like to be near water. The male and female birds circle about their homes, swooping and rising and twittering constantly. Sometimes the female perches on top of the house and the male hovers or flutters in small circles above her. At other times, both birds sit on the house and bow to one another. These "flutter-flights" and "bowing" activities are part of their courtship displays.

Egg laying begins in early June and the female alone incubates them. However, the male remains about the house and guards the entrance when the female leaves to feed. The young hatch in mid June and both parents carry food to them. The young leave the nest in early July, but remain in the area for a few days and often perch on the fence where their parents continue feeding them.

After nesting, the tree swallows range widely over the dykelands and are joined along the river by bank and barn swallows. The tree swallows start congregating in August and, by mid month, flocks of one or two hundred birds perch, evenly spaced, on the wires along the highway. Most tree swallows leave by late August, although a few linger and occasionally sail over the meadows until late October.

The upper portion of the meadow is drier and is covered with grass and a variety of wildflowers, and we planted a hedge of multiflora rose and a copse of evergreen trees along the border of the property. Savannah and chipping sparrows live on the drier parts of the meadow in summer, and kingbirds use fence posts and tree tops for lookout perches. Both sparrows arrive in early May, and are seen on most walks from then until late September. They flit through the rose bushes and perch on the fence, and the chipping sparrows often forage on the path. The savannahs nest on the ground, in deep grass along the fence, while the chipping sparrows often nest on the lower branches of a multiflora rose that grows up through a young white pine tree.

Tree Swallows

Tree Swallow

Sparrows and Kingbirds

Chipping Sparrow

107

Kingbird

Kingbirds are on the meadow from late May until mid September, and groups of eight to twelve birds may visit briefly during migration in late August. They nest in June in the trees or shrubs that border the river, and by late July two or three young are often perched along the fence where their parents feed them. Kingbirds, noted for their aggressiveness, attack any bird that intrudes into their territories and treat large and small birds alike. They dive at and pester the intruder until it leaves. Kingbirds attack singly, in pairs or groups, and may team up with other species. One August day a few years ago, we watched six kingbirds and four barn swallows chase a female harrier from the meadow and far across neighbouring fields.

Waxwings

Flocks of cedar waxwings may visit the meadow at any time during the summer and autumn, and occasionally in winter. They nest in the wild rose bushes. Waxwings are nomadic birds and appear whenever food is available. Their lisping chatter announces their arrival as the flock circles and drops down into the bushes and trees. Waxwings feed on berries and seeds, or dart out like flycatchers to catch insects, and do so without interrupting their continuous chattering. Many birds chatter or utter call-notes when travelling in flocks. It is a means of recognition and helps keep the flock together.

Each waxwing is reddish-brown and has a crested head with black markings, and a grayish tail tipped with yellow. When the bird is perched, the crest and the bird's upright posture are features that help identify it from a distance. The name describes the reddish, wax-like beads that many have on their wing feathers. The significance of these beads is not known. Presumably they have a social value, perhaps providing a means for individual recognition.

November 9, 1980, was another "first" day for our garden list. We had just started across the meadow when we saw a flock of eighteen waxwings sitting in the rose thickets and adjacent trees. They were larger and grayer than cedar waxwings. When we got closer, the white wing-bars and deep reddish, undertail markings confirmed their identification as Bohemian waxwings. These birds were described as "irregular" winter visitors to Nova Scotia

Cedar Waxwing

at that time. However, their visits have become more frequent and flocks numbering up to 300 birds now visit The Old Place. They visit several times during most winters and stay in the area for a week or two each time.

Undisturbed meadows and fields are required if ground-nesting birds are to survive about our homes and communities. It is difficult to imagine a spring without the cheerful songs of bobolinks and the winnowing sounds of snipe. Uncut fields and wide borders around wetlands and along rivers are needed. Both can be provided by land owners and communities.

Undisturbed Places

BEYOND THE NORTH WIND

Bird migration is a fascinating topic. The timing and distances travelled make it remarkable. Waterfowl and shorebirds congregate at specific staging areas precisely at times of food abundance, and they complete nesting in the short period before cold weather reduces their food supplies. This dependence on specific sites and food resources, however, makes these species vulnerable. Loss of staging sites, disturbance, or contamination of food supplies can destroy entire populations. These sites must be protected with care. While this requires international cooperation, communities and individual land owners are the primary stewards of the migration routes. They can establish protected areas and keep the feeding and roosting sites clean.

Geese and shorebirds, at times in huge flocks, visit the Minas Basin and surrounding farm fields during migration. They are migrating between their southern wintering areas and their northern nesting sites, some in the far north. Their visits are highlights on the local nature calendar.

Geese

A few Canada geese return in mid March, but the major flights arrive in early April and their numbers increase to about 10,000 birds by mid April. We were birding on the dykelands a few years ago when a major flock arrived. We heard them first, and soon spotted the dark, noisy cloud of geese far to the west. We watched as they approached, flying steadily and "honking" continuously; and we watched as skein after skein passed overhead and glided down to alight in the mouth of the river. It took a full ten minutes for all of them to fly past and settle on the water.

Their characteristic "V" and "J" flight patterns and their loud honking and chattering are familiar sights and sounds at The Old Place each spring. The geese are migrating to their nesting sites in Newfoundland and Labrador, and some continue to Hudson Bay and the Ungava Peninsula. Those that arrive first are probably the birds that spend the winter in sheltered coves along the outer coast of Nova Scotia and move onto the dykelands when the snow begins to melt. Later, flocks from along the coast of New England arrive, and are followed still later by geese that overwin-

A Flight of Geese

ter as far south as the Carolinas and Florida.

We always check flocks of Canada geese for snow geese. Snow geese are only occasional visitors to this area. The nearest migration route passes to the west across Maine and along the upper St. Lawrence River Valley. However, we find one or two snow geese among the Canada geese most years, and suspect that these flocks are from the Carolinas and Florida where the two species spend the winter together.

One April a few years ago, we found a record number of eight snow geese in a flock of 400 Canadas. These birds foraged in the fields behind The Old Place and remained here for about two weeks. Each morning, at about 8:30, we could look out the window and watch the skeins of geese gliding down to alight on the river and adjacent fields, with the eight snow geese together within a "V" of Canadas.

The older species name for the snow goose was *hyperborea*. It is not used now, but we prefer that name for it translates into "beyond the north wind" and is an appropriate name for a bird that flies to the high Arctic to nest. Some snow geese nest as far north as the Queen Elizabeth Islands!

Snow Goose

In the evening, just after dusk, the geese fly to the Basin, often with the flocks having congregated into a dark and noisy cloud that drifts along the horizon in the dim light. On some April evenings, we sit by the river just to watch this fly-past and to listen to the strange but wonderful sounds of their voices. Some fly so close to us that we can hear the whistling and swishing sounds of their wings. Each morning they return to forage on farm fields.

On the Basin, the geese usually rest near the entrance of a freshwater river, and there is often a raft of up to a thousand birds just off the Habitant River. Geese are less able to excrete salt than are sea ducks, for their salt glands are not as highly developed. Possibly this is why they prefer the water of lower salinities found near river mouths.

Fewer geese stop here during fall migration, with the flocks together totalling only about 2000 birds. They start to arrive in mid September and some remain until snow blankets the fields in December. In early autumn, we see flocks of ten to twen-

Canada Geese

ty birds flying inland. These are the explorers searching for the best fields on which to forage. On subsequent days, the flocks gradually increase in size as additional geese are guided to the choice fields, and by mid autumn some flocks have increased to a few hundred birds. The geese also fly into the fields to forage during the bright moonlight of the Harvest Moon. They forage in fields of corn stubble where there are waste ears and kernels, in potato fields where the smaller potatoes were left behind by the harvester, and in fields of recently harvested grain. In late fall, after the ground freezes, the geese move to fields of newly emerged winter rye and to mowed or cattle-grazed fields where they feed on the shoots of grass and clover that are only a few centimetres high.

Geese wearing collars are occasionally present in the flocks. Researchers place these collars on the geese. The collars have large numbers that can be read with a telescope and the researchers, in return for reports of sightings, provide information about the bird. A goose wearing collar number YBJ05P was banded in New Jersey on March 1, 1984, and was subsequently seen in New Jersey (Oct. 2/84), Quebec (April 20/86), New Jersey (Jan. 8/87), and Nova Scotia (Nov. 21/87).

By collaring and following a large number of geese, information is gathered on the size of populations, use of habitat and food, and the effects of hunting. As a result of these studies, we know that there has been an overall increase in the number of geese in the Atlantic Flyway during the past fifty years, although it has declined during the past few years. Several years of deep snows in the north that reduced nesting success probably contributed to this decline. Recording such changes in numbers gives a basis for adjustments in conservation practices, and emphasizes the value of an ongoing monitoring programme.

However, the goose population has grown over the longer term. This growth was a by-product of farmers increasing the acreage planted in grain, and was assisted by interested individuals and communities establishing preserves along the migration routes and in overwintering areas. It is a good example of how individuals and communities working together can help build and maintain a wildlife population.

Like geese, many of our shorebird visitors also nest under the north wind, although few go as far north as do the northern-most snow geese. Huge numbers visit the Minas Basin during their southward migration when some two million birds forage on the tidal flats. The upper Bay of Fundy including the Minas Basin is one of only a few staging sites for these species in the world. They begin to arrive in mid July and reach peak numbers in early August. Individual flocks may number over a hundred thousand birds, and the precision with which they fly and turn and dip in unison is marvelous to watch. More than twenty species of shore-birds visit here each summer.

The Minas Basin has been a staging area for migrating shorebirds for a long time. They were described in 1882 by Bernard Gilpin, a well-known naturalist of that time: "The most obvious, and those from which numbers and from sight most modify our landscape, are the sand peeps, and next them the ring necks. These two speck the feathery margins of our salt-estuaries, whitening our flats and flashing like silver clouds in the air. Next in number come the larger plover, the golden and beetle heads… The whole host, scared by your approaching canoe, with a sharp whistle rise, stretch landward a few rods, then rise in the air and open into a white sparkling cloud, reflecting the bright sun-beams." Today, semipalmated sandpipers (sand peeps) number well into the hundreds of thousands, semipalmated (ring necks) and black-bellied (beetle heads) plovers are abundant, and flocks of up to forty golden-plovers forage on the dykelands.

At high tide the shorebirds fly inland to roost on farm fields. Black-bellied plovers often roost on the meadow at The Old Place. Twenty to thirty black-bellied plovers visit here each May. They are one of only a few shorebirds to stop during their migra-tion north. However, they return in much larger numbers in mid summer when migrating to their wintering areas in South and Central Americas. While here, they forage for marine organisms on the tidal flats and for grasshoppers and other insects on farm fields. At The Old Place, they fly into the meadow in small groups or in flocks of up to a hundred birds, turning and circling in uni-son, and calling "pee-u-wee" plaintively and repeatedly as they glide down onto the field.

Shorebirds

Black-bellied Plover

Semipalmated Sandpiper

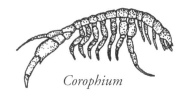

Corophium

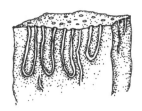

Corophium tubes in sand

Large numbers of shorebirds roost on neighbouring farm fields and we watch wave after wave of them flying over The Old Place. The short-billed dowitchers are the first to fly over, heading inland about two hours before high tide. The flocks of semipalmated sandpipers begin to fly over about an hour later. This pattern simply reflects the distribution of these birds on the tidal flats. The dowitchers feed primarily on marine worms on the outer flats that are flooded first by the rising tide. The beds of crustaceans where the sandpipers congregate are located on the inner flats and are flooded later. Regular surveys of neighbouring farm fields to locate shorebird roosts are an important part of the birding routine for August and early September.

By far the most numerous shorebirds to visit the Minas Basin are the semipalmated sandpipers. They stop here to feed on marine organisms on the tidal flats and build up the energy reserves needed for the next lap of their southward migration. In particular, they feed on a crustacean called *Corophium*, the mud shrimp. *Corophium* is about one centimetre long and lives in a U-shaped tube that it builds in the upper seven centimetres of the sand. The arrival of the shorebirds coincides with a peak in the reproductive cycle of *Corophium,* when counts of up to 20,000 shrimp, and occasionally to 50,000, per square metre are recorded. Each flock of sandpipers remains for ten days to two weeks, and individual birds may double their body weight, from about 22 grams to over 44 grams, during that time. As flocks leave to continue their migration, others arrive from the north and west, and large numbers of sandpipers are present until early September.

Semipalmated sandpipers follow a precise migration cycle. Most winter at Suriname on the northern coast of South America, nest in the Arctic, and congregate in between at staging areas to rest and store up the energy needed to continue their journey. They follow two major routes north from Suriname. On one route, the sandpipers stop to feed at Cheyenne Bottoms in Kansas; on the other route, they forage at Delaware Bay in New Jersey. Their stop at Delaware Bay coincides with a massive spawning of horseshoe crabs and the birds feast on the eggs. The sandpipers then continue their flight to the Arctic, stopping to feed along the many ponds and potholes on the prairies. When nesting is completed, they congregate about Hudson Bay and from there fly to the upper Bay of Fundy and Minas Basin. After feeding here, they make a non-stop flight of several thousand kilometres to South America, completing their migratory cycle. This flight is over water and, flying high and assisted by the winds, takes three to five days.

The precise timing of this cycle and the enormous number of birds in such small areas surely qualifies it as one of the wonders of nature. It is also frightening. What would happen to these sandpipers if the shores of Delaware Bay or the Minas Basin became contaminated, if the prairie potholes were drained, or the Hudson Bay marshes were altered by development projects? Where would these birds build the reserves needed for the next lap of their migration? Fortunately, the Western Hemispheric Shorebird Reserve Network programme is attempting to protect the staging areas, and the southern bight of the Minas Basin is included in that programme.

A late night visit to the meadow in mid August is another highlight on our nature calendar. The sky is spectacular. The stars are brilliant, the Milky Way appears like a whitish arch across the sky and, under the arch, the fiery trails of the Perseid meteors streak in all directions from the northeast. Far below, the water laps quietly among the reeds along the river, and from high overhead we hear the sounds of sandpipers as flock after flock leave on the next leg of their southward migration. A clear night in mid August is one of nature's treats.

Nature's Treat

Migrating birds command special interest and must receive special care, for entire breeding populations may be concentrated at a few critical locations. They require nesting, feeding, roosting and wintering sites that are free from contamination and disturbance. Communities and land owners can provide and protect the required sites.

Community Preserves

MEADOW IN BLOOM

Wild fields provide magnificent displays of colour. They also provide cover for small mammals, nesting sites and materials for birds, summer and winter food supplies for many animals, and host plants for butterflies, bees and other insects. However, wild fields are disappearing as construction, cultivation and grazing advance. Communities and land owners can set fields and wide borders aside and allow them to remain wild. Collectively, this would help to preserve a unique environment for the many creatures that depend on it, and the annual displays of colour and the cycles of birds and other animals would continue for everyone to enjoy.

The white blossoms of shadbush and then multiflora rose are among the first flowers on the meadow each spring, and are followed by yellow dandelions. There are clusters of white and yellow daisies in early summer, and the white flowers of wild strawberries promise handfuls of sweet berries in July. In mid summer there are patchworks of reddish sheep sorrel, blue tangles of vetch, yellow hawkweed and white Queen Anne's lace. As summer progresses, cinquefoil turns yellow and the clovers form red and white carpets. Late summer and autumn bring the white and blues of asters, the blues of thistles, and the yellows of goldenrods and tansies. The meadow is filled with wildflowers and the displays of colour change continuously.

Shrubs   There is a shadbush in the centre of the meadow at The Old Place. It is a small tree and is inconspicuous for much of the year, but in mid May its white blossoms provide a glorious contrast to the unfolding greens of springtime. Its flowers provide an important source of pollen and nectar for the insects of early spring. The flower clusters are near the ends of the branches and often appear at the same time that the leaves begin to unfold. The young leaves are sometimes an attractive bronze, making the white flowers even more conspicuous. In autumn, the leaves turn to colourful shades of amber and purple.

Shadbush berries mature in early summer. They are purplish red, juicy, sweet and edible. The settlers, and especially the early explorers and trappers, used shadbush berries when making pemmican. Following the practice of the native people, these high-energy cakes were made by mixing the berries with meat and fat. Today the berries are still used to make jams and jellies, but they must be picked promptly for they are also favourites of pheasants, starlings, catbirds and robins.

It is called shadbush because it blooms when shad move into the rivers to spawn. Indian pear and wild pear are also common names and refer to its fleshy fruits that were once gathered in large quantities for food. Lescarbot described this shrub in 1609 when he wrote: "In the woods I have seen there small pears very delicate". It has other names: Juneberry, because its fruit begins to ripen and may be picked in June; salmonberry, because it blooms when the young salmon are moving down the rivers to the sea; and serviceberry, according to one explanation, because it blooms at the end of winter when in older times the clergy could again visit rural communities and conduct religious services.

We allowed multiflora roses to grow wild over much of the north half of the original hayfield and create a thick tangle that provides both shelter and food for wildlife. Song sparrows live in the rose thickets all year and sing from the tall wands, yellow warblers nest there in summer, and one or two mockingbirds arrive in October and remain within the dense shrubbery throughout the winter. The tangles are home through the seasons to pheasants, catbirds, waxwings, robins and purple finches.

In early summer these roses flood the inner meadow with a sea of white blossoms, and in winter the young growth and hips are red. This is where we counted 173 robins one day in mid February during a fall of soft, fluffy snow. They belonged to a northern race and had come south to overwinter in the more moderate climate of Nova Scotia. The rose thickets provided a welcoming food supply and the robins remained until spring.

Ox-eye daisies begin flowering in mid June and continue through early August, and clusters of their bright white and yellow blossoms are abundant on the meadow. Daisies are not native plants. They were brought here by the settlers, perhaps as garden

Shadbush

Flowers of Early Summer

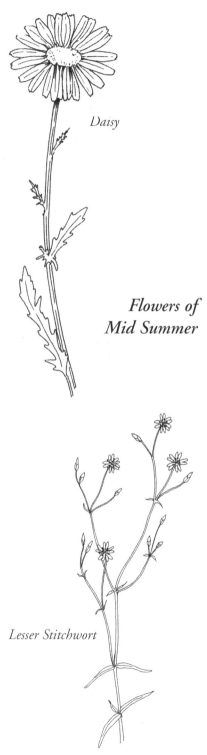

Daisy

**Flowers of
Mid Summer**

Lesser Stitchwort

flowers or mixed with hay seed, and have since spread widely and are now one of our common field flowers.

Daisies grow where the grass is sufficiently sparse to permit them to reach through to the light. A number of plant clusters may grow from the same underground stem, and some clusters number up to thirty flower-heads. The name "daisy" is a shortened form of "day's eye", for each opens with the sunrise and closes in the evening.

Each flower-head is composed of many small flowers of two types: pistillate ray-flowers along the periphery and disc-flowers with both pistils and stamens in the centre. An insect usually alights at the edge where it deposits pollen on the ray-flowers. It then circles toward the centre and collects new pollen from the disc- flowers to carry to the next daisy it visits.

We enjoy watching a number of flowering plants in summer. Lesser stitchwort and blue vetch form thick tangles, and the individual plants of Queen Anne's lace stand tall along the path. Lesser stitchwort grows like a fine vine through the uncut grass. Its flowers are small and white, with each petal cleft almost to its base. Stitchwort provides a profusion of blossoms from early summer to mid autumn, and an abundance of seeds in late autumn and winter for sparrows and finches.

Vetch is also a trailing plant, reaching up to a metre in length. It grows through the grass and creeps up bushes and young trees. Vetch is most noticeable when it begins to blossom in early July and forms large, blue patches scattered over the meadow. Each leaf is made up of several leaflets and ends in two or three tendrils. When a tendril touches a stalk of grass or a bush, it curls around it and then coils to pull the leaf around so that the two become firmly entwined. Vetch is not a native plant but was introduced from Europe, presumably mixed with hay seed, as were many plants that grow on the landward side of the dykes.

Vetch has a curiously-shaped flower, one typical of all beans and peas and described as having the shape of a butterfly. Each flower has a broad upper petal, two side petals or "wings", and two lower petals that form a "keel" enclosing the stamens and pistil. The bee alights on the keel, pushing it down and exposing the stamens and pistil so that pollination can occur and new pollen can be picked up to be carried to the next flower. When the bee leaves, the keel lifts again to enclose and protect the reproductive organs.

The flowers of vetch are clustered along one side of a spike with the older flowers near the base and the younger flowers near the top. By mid summer, the basal flowers have been fertilized and are wilting, those in the mid portion are blue and mature and ready to be pollinated, and those at the tip are pink and still developing. Like other legumes, the seeds form in a pod that, when mature in late summer, snaps open with a twist to expel the seeds.

As with peas, beans and clover, the roots of vetch possess numerous white nodules. These contain a type of bacteria that captures nitrogen from the air in the soil and converts it to nitrate. In this way, vetch helps enrich the soils of the meadow for all plants, and is sometimes planted as a ground-cover in gardens and agricultural fields for this purpose.

Vetch

Queen Anne's lace, or wild carrot, borders the path along the drier parts of the meadow. It blossoms from July to September, and has flat-topped clusters of creamy white flowers. The individual flowers are tiny, with five petals, and are arranged in groups that form a radial pattern about a central group. It is this pattern that gives the flower clusters the appearance of lace. One story suggests that this plant grew in the royal gardens at the time of Queen Anne and that she used it as a pattern when making lace.

The leaves are finely divided and fern-like, and another story claims that ladies in the time of Queen Anne wore them to decorate their hair. Today they are widely used in floral arrangements. The leaves, when crushed, smell like carrots and the root is a long tap root, also like that of a carrot, although white. The vegetable is a variety of Queen Anne's lace.

Queen Anne's Lace

Queen Anne's lace is not a native plant, but was brought here by the early settlers who planted it in their kitchen gardens for ornamental and herbal uses. A carrot-flavoured tea may be made from its seeds and dried leaves. It was also valued for medicinal purposes for, as is now known of carrots, it has a high content of vitamin A. Queen Anne's lace escaped from the early gardens, and was likely introduced with hay seed as well, and is now a common plant in old fields and other dry sites.

Flowers of Late Summer

Four species of white and blue asters are common and form wide borders along the meadow path. They flower in late summer and autumn. Heart-leafed aster grows on the drier and sunnier parts of the meadow. Its leaves are heart-shaped and its flowers have blue, occasionally white, petals surrounding reddish discs. New York aster grows in wetter and shadier sites. Its leaves are lance-shaped and its flowers range from deep violet to a purplish colour. Flat-topped white aster and calico aster have white flowers. Those of flat-topped aster are large and arranged at the ends of the stems. Those of calico aster are smaller and grow from the leaf axils. Both are tall plants and grow in moist, shaded places.

Our favourite flower of late summer and autumn is touch-me-not or jewelweed. It grows to well over a metre in height and forms large stands that spread over the moist soil under the trees on the inner meadow. Touch-me-not begins to flower in late July, but the full displays are not exhibited until August. The flowers are orange with reddish-brown speckles. Each flower is bell-shaped with a circle of petals in front and a curved spur in back, and each dangles on a short stem like a jewel. The leaves are oval and green, and appear silvery when moistened with the dew of early morning. The long seed capsules suddenly burst when ripe and throw their seeds a distance of a metre or more away from the plant. The ripe seed capsules also burst when touched, thus the name "touch-me-not".

Touch-me-not

Touch-me-not is a favourite not only because of its flower displays, but also because its nectar attracts hummingbirds. Touch-me-nots begin flowering at the same time as young hummingbirds are leaving their nests and learning the techniques of foraging on their own. We have counted as many as fifteen hummingbirds in the touch-me-nots at one time, and we spend a considerable amount of time watching and enjoying them.

Flower Walk

One value of walking the same path on a regular basis is the enjoyment derived from anticipating and discovering the "new" flowers that appear through the seasons. Watching the annual cycles of plants growing, flowers unfolding, seeds developing and plants dying back enhances our appreciation of nature. The colours on the meadow change constantly and the succession is an ongoing source of pleasure — well worth the decision to keep a "wild" meadow.

WINTER MEADOW

Animals require shelters and good food supplies to survive the winter. Wild fields, wide borders and hedgerows provide both. Cultivated fields and mowed areas lack seed plants and thick undergrowth. This again emphasizes the need for communities and land owners to set aside fields and wide borders and allow them to remain wild.

The winter meadow appears to be a harsh environment, quite different from the summer one. Snow, freezing rains, ice, drying winds and cold temperatures impose severe conditions for survival. However, the meadow provides the basic needs of food and shelter and plants and animals respond in different ways to the various demands of winter.

The main features seen about the meadow while cross-country skiing are the large patches of dried plants and the flocks of birds that feed on their seeds. The taller plants stand above the snow, as do tufts of grass, but identifying them is sometimes a challenge. At ground level, under the snow and protected by its warm blanket, many plants remain alive and green throughout winter.

A Seed Supply

Asters, goldenrods and tansies form extensive beds. They are composites and their numerous flowers collectively produce an enormous number of seeds. Cinquefoil also produces large numbers of seeds. It is easy to recognize, for its stalk gives rise to a number of loosely arranged branches, each of which ends in a round seed capsule. Similarly, the branches of knapweed end in round seed capsules. The seed capsules of evening primrose are oval in shape, with each split into four "petals" that curl back like a dried flower. The flower-heads of Queen Anne's lace are distinctive. In late summer and autumn, they dry and curl up to form cups or "bird nests". In winter these bird nests fill with snow and are quite attractive. Under the snow, the leaves of Queen Anne's lace are green and finely divided. The leaves of yarrow are similar, but are highly fragrant and the groups of dried flowers form flat-topped clusters. All of these plants, and others, produce an abun-

Winter Plants

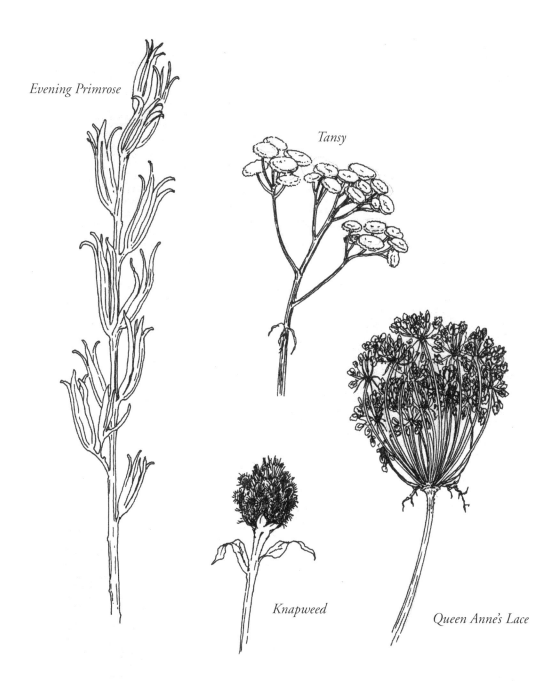

Evening Primrose

Tansy

Knapweed

Queen Anne's Lace

dant supply of seeds that attracts a variety of sparrows and finches to the winter meadow.

Surviving the Cold

Plants survive cold weather in different ways. In general, they become dormant and growth stops when temperatures drop, although a low level of photosynthesis may continue especially when a covering of snow protects the leaves. "Hardening" is the process that prepares plants for cold temperatures. It is initiated by the decreased daylight hours of early autumn, while the leaves are still active. Decreased daylight stimulates the leaves to produce a hormone that is transported throughout the plant. Later, with the colder temperatures and water shortages of autumn, this hormone promotes the hardening process. It takes several days for a plant to "harden off", and an early frost before hardening is completed may damage or kill the plant although the temperatures are still warmer than those it will survive in winter. Similarly, in spring the hardened state is lost as the weather warms, after which a late frost may injure the plant.

Hardening includes several changes in cells that enable the plant to survive the cold. The sugar and protein content of the cells and sap increases and lowers the point at which they freeze by several degrees. The lipid content also changes. Lipids are components of cell membranes and are critical to cell activity. Some lipids solidify quickly at cool temperatures, whereas others remain fluid. Part of the hardening process includes a build up of the chill-resistant lipids, and this maintains membrane function. In such ways, the plant is able to delay the onset of freezing and even to avoid freezing at moderately low temperatures.

It is the internal formation of ice at low temperatures that damages the plant. Plants do freeze, but the effects are minimized by reducing the water content of the tissues and by limiting the size of the ice crystals. Tissues lose water during the period of frost hardening, and additional water is drawn out of the cells as ice forms around them. The ice forms only on the outside of the cells where it does not interfere with the cells' low rate of metabolism. Also, plants produce antifreeze proteins that prevent the growth of large ice crystals. By reducing water content and producing antifreezes, plants reduce the likelihood that small ice crystals will grow into large ones and damage their cells and tissues.

Winter brings species of birds to the meadow that are different from those present in summer. They are attracted by the abundance of seeds and by the insects associated with seed-producing plants. Many of these birds nest in the north, some near the tree line and others on the tundra. They migrate south in winter and join resident species in areas that offer a good food supply. Flocks of tree sparrows, juncos, goldfinches, horned larks, snow buntings and occasionally redpolls forage on the meadow. These birds prefer weedy fields and hedgerows and do not frequent woodlands. Without the seed plants, there would be few birds on the meadow in winter.

At night and during inclement weather, winter birds seek the shelter of coniferous trees and rose thickets, and some burrow into hummocks of grass or into the snow. Like many birds, they conserve heat by growing additional feathers in cold weather and by "fluffing-out" their feathers to trap a layer of warm air next to their bodies. They also consume extra food and maintain a high level of metabolism to generate additional heat. In such ways, these birds are able to protect themselves from the cold.

Tree sparrows are the first of the northern birds to arrive at The Old Place. A few come in late October and by early December there are one or two dozen about the bushes and dried flower stalks. Although mixed with goldfinches and juncos, their chestnut-coloured caps, white wing-bars, and the single dark "button" in the middle of the breast make their identification an easy task.

Tree sparrows usually forage in bushes or on the ground. They search for seeds about flower-heads, pick up seeds that have fallen on the snow, and jump up to shake other seeds off the plants. They also frequent the feeders about the house, especially those offering white millet and Niger seeds. At night and during stormy weather, tree sparrows sometimes burrow into hummocks of grass for shelter from the wind and cold.

Common redpolls are numerous about The Old Place some winters and absent during others. They live and nest along the tree line in the north but migrate south in winters when there

Winter Birds

Tree Sparrow

Redpoll

Snow Bunting

is a shortage of seeds at home. Redpolls are the size of small sparrows. They are brownish birds with conspicuous red caps. The males also have reddish breasts. They arrive in flocks that may number up to 200 birds and feed on seeds in the field and about the birch trees. Here, as in other communities, large numbers also come to the feeders on the lawn and windowsill, especially those with Niger seed.

Like other birds, redpolls survive low temperatures by "fluffing-out" their feathers and roosting in the shelter of coniferous trees. In addition, each redpoll has a "pocket" inside its throat, just behind the mouth, and stores extra food in it while feeding during the late afternoon. When roosting at night, the redpoll eats these seeds and obtains the energy needed to protect it from the cold.

Snow buntings, also called snowbirds and snowflakes, are favourite visitors. They are generally white, with some rust colouring, and their wings and tails are black with white patches. They become whiter during the course of the winter as the rust-coloured tips of their feathers are worn off. Snow buntings nest in northern Labrador and the Arctic, but move south each winter. They arrive along our coast in October and many move onto farm fields and dykelands once the snow begins to accumulate in December. At night and during inclement weather, buntings take shelter in hummocks of grass, or they may burrow into the snow where, only a few centimetres deep, it may be ten degrees warmer than the air above.

Buntings travel in flocks that number from a few to one or two hundred birds. The flock drifts across the field, with the birds wheeling in unison, flashing white wings and undersides and tumbling down to the ground like a cloud of whirling snowflakes. Sometimes buntings surround us when we ski across the dykelands and, if we stand quietly, they scamper over the snow about our skis. Buntings hop from one seed plant to the next, with the birds in the rear flying over to alight in front of the flock. Each twitters constantly, as described by John Burroughs, "in a voice of good cheer and contentment".

While patches of plants and flocks of birds are the obvious features of the meadow in winter, there are other signs of living things. Although less conspicuous, they also illustrate ways in which animals survive cold temperatures. Insects are not easily observed in winter, but galls, webs, wasp's nests, rolled leaves and cocoons reveal their presence. Galls are common and can easily be found with a little searching. They occur on many plants, and are often numerous on goldenrod.

Goldenrod galls appear as large swellings on plant stems that result from localized areas of abnormal growth. They are caused by insects seeking the food and shelter needed to survive the winter. There are two types of galls on goldenrod. One is spindle-shaped and is caused by the goldenrod gall moth, a small moth with pointed wings. The second type is round. It is the common one and is caused by a small fruit fly with beautifully marked wings.

The female goldenrod gall moth lays eggs on the plant in autumn and the caterpillars hatch in spring. The young caterpillars feed on the new growth and burrow into the stems. This stimulates growth of the plant tissues around the caterpillar to form the gall. Within the gall in mid summer, the caterpillar gradually changes into a moth and in early autumn, about a year after the egg was laid, the fully formed moth emerges from the gall and flies away. In winter, these galls have a tiny hole near the top through which the moth escaped. A variety of small insects and spiders live in these empty galls and chickadees hunt through the patches of goldenrod to feed on them.

The round galls, on the other hand, contain an overwintering larva and, as yet, do not have an escape hole. The female fly lays eggs on the goldenrod in spring. The eggs hatch and the larvae burrow into the stem. The plant responds to the irritation by forming a gall around each larva. The larva overwinters within the gall and, the following spring, develops into an adult fly and escapes from the gall. We often see downy woodpeckers about patches of goldenrod, for the gall larvae are one of their favourite winter foods.

Overwintering insects also have mechanisms that enable them to survive freezing temperatures. In autumn, stimulated by

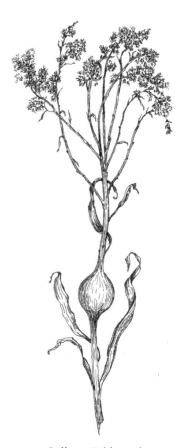

Gall on Goldenrod

lower temperatures, insects begin to manufacture antifreeze chemicals that accumulate within their tissues. Glycerol is one of these antifreezes. It lowers the freezing point of the body fluids, and enables the insect to endure low temperatures. It also limits the growth of small ice crystals into large crystals that would damage the insect's tissues.

Winter Mammals

Small mammals are common on the meadow in summer, and some are active all winter while others hibernate. Meadow voles remain active and their tunnels under a light snow or a thin coating of ice provide evidence of life on the winter meadow. Other mammals, like the meadow jumping mouse, hibernate during winter.

The meadow jumping mouse lives in areas of thick grass and bushes. It prefers moist habitats with tall flowers, and is present in damp areas of the meadow where asters and touch-me-nots are abundant. The meadow jumping mouse has long hind legs and a very long tail. It usually travels by taking short hops, but can take long jumps when startled. Jumping mice build summer nests in hummocks of grass and in brush piles, but they build their winter nests below ground where the temperature is warmer and less variable than on the surface. At a depth of about twenty centimetres, for example, the temperature remains fairly constant at -4° C. Jumping mice store fat during late summer, enter hibernation in late autumn, and do not emerge again until May. During hibernation their breathing rate, heart beat and body temperature are lowered. They use little energy and the stored fat provides the nourishment needed. Within the winter nest, this low level of metabolism is sufficient to generate the heat needed to keep from freezing.

The storage and accumulation of fat in animals during periods of feeding are well-known processes. However, many mammals, perhaps all and including some birds, have a second type of fat tissue that is not related to feeding. It is called brown fat because it contains a large amount of brown pigment. Brown fat produces heat rather than stores nourishment, and the associated blood vessels are arranged so that the blood carries this heat directly to the brain, heart, lungs and kidneys. This type of fat is

Meadow Jumping Mouse

especially well developed in hibernating mammals. In spring, the metabolism of this fat provides heat to the vital organs and initiates the arousal process.

A meadow or field appears to be a desolate place in winter, but a variety of living things can be found with careful observation. These plants and animals exhibit a number of interesting adaptations and behaviours that enables each to survive the drying winds and cold temperatures. Shelter and food are required for survival and both are provided by wild fields and wide borders. Can you or your community allow a field to remain wild? Also, sowing wild flowers in vacant lots, along highways and traffic interchanges will collectively help conserve these habitats.

Wild Field and Borders Needed

However, in many regions wild fields originate as the result of human activity, often from unused farm fields, more so than from natural processes. Unless maintained, they quickly fill with shrubs and trees and revert to woodland. Nevertheless, wild fields have been a part of our landscape for almost three centuries and many species of plants and animals have become associated with them and dependent on them. We may have to cut wild fields every few years to keep these plants and animals about our communities. But they should be cut in spring before seed plants start to grow and birds start to nest, and with cutters set high to limit disturbance of the undergrowth. Wild fields are well worth the minimal effort needed to keep them. Many people will enjoy listening to the birds singing in spring, discovering the colourful displays of flowers and butterflies in summer, and watching the flocks of winter birds wheeling and tumbling into the patches of seed plants.

Maintainng Wild Fields

WOODLAND GARDEN

"These are my gates of wonder…"
The Fir Wood
Charles G.D. Roberts, 1889.

WOODLAND PATH

In planning your community, are you planting trees for future generations? Can you set aside an area of trees and allow them to reach their full size? Can you conserve a woodlot and allow it to progress to a stable forest? Planting a tree is a selfless act, for you plant for the next generation and not for yourself. If future generations are to enjoy the grandeur of old trees, you will have to plant them and your community will have to care for them. Nature stewardship is based on selfless acts.

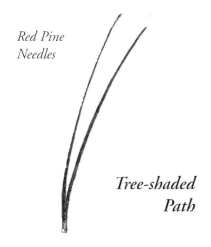

Red Pine Needles

Tree-shaded Path

Red Pine Cone

The woodland path leads west from the front driveway, and then curves down the hill and crosses the marsh to join the path around the meadow. It is a tree-shaded avenue with thick shrubbery forming the understory. The woodland path introduces us to a tremendous number of living things, for even dead trees are full of life. It offers the challenges of finding spring flowers, recognizing birds in autumn colours, and identifying trees and shrubs in winter. However, while we enjoy the flowers, birds and trees, an understanding of soil and soil organisms is basic to maintaining a healthy woodland, as well as other ecosystems.

Red and white pines grow along the woodland path. They are tall trees and their branches form part of the canopy that shades the understory. Both pines provide food for wildlife. Many birds, such as chickadees and siskins, eat the seeds, and squirrels and mice eat both seeds and buds. A hundred years and more ago, magnificent stands of tall, straight pines grew in this area, with white pine growing on the moist loam along the tidal marsh and red pine on the drier and sandier uplands. They made masts from these pines in the days of wooden-ship building. Such stands are now hard to find.

White and red spruces also grow in the woodland. Especially in winter, chickadees, kinglets and red-breasted nuthatches constantly flit among the cones at the tops of these trees, and search through the needles and over the bark for mites and insect eggs. In years when there is a good cone crop, small flocks of white-winged crossbills visit and stay for several days. In winter, the snow weighs down the lower boughs of these trees, "roofing-in" spaces around the trunks. A number of small mammals and birds, and especially pheasants, take shelter from winter storms and low temperatures in these "tents".

White spruce was probably scarce in the area of The Old Place when the settlers arrived. It is a tree of the early stages of forest succession and would not have been a major part of a stable woodland. Now it flourishes on abandoned fields and is one of the first trees to invade such sites. In turn, species such as maple and ash seed-in under the spruces and gradually grow taller and shade them. Spruces are not tolerant of shade and are soon replaced by these other trees.

Sugar and red maples are present in the woodland. The sugar maples, tall and highly branched with rounded crowns, are dominant trees in stable woods. Grosbeaks feed on maple seeds and buds, warblers and vireos search for insects among the leaves, and thrushes nest in the lower branches. Both maples flower in early spring. The flowers are small and clustered at the ends of the branches, and the hanging, yellowish flowers of sugar maples and the deep red flowers of red maples colour the woodland path. Similarly, maples contribute to the striking colours of autumn, when the golds of sugar maples stand out against the reds of red maples, the yellows of elms and the smoky purples of ashes.

Some old trees, often elms and maples, were planted more than a hundred years ago to mark property boundaries. These farms extended from the valley up the mountain "to a point from which a man can carry wood down". There, they bordered on mountain lots that extended down "to a point from which a man can carry wood up". (Such 1880 deed descriptions must challenge modern surveyors!) While many boundary trees have died or been cut, the pattern of some early farms as marked by the trees can still be pictured from the top of the mountain.

We do not remove trees when they die, provided they are in a place where they will do no harm when they fall and there is no danger of disease spreading to other trees. Rather, we watch the succession of plants and animals that becomes associated with

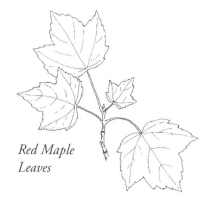

Red Maple Leaves

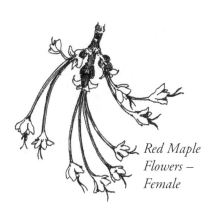

Red Maple Flowers – Female

Red Maple Flowers – Male

Life in Dead Trees

them. Many organisms live in association with dead wood.

Boring insects and bark beetles attack dead trees and open them up to invasions by fungi. These actions are important first steps in the decomposition of wood. The softened wood may then be chiseled and shredded by a variety of animals as they search for insects. Decomposing wood is a good substrate on which other plants and fungi grow.

The bark beetles, only three or four millimetres long and with short antennae, bore into the inner bark. They gain entrance by chewing small round holes, and this has earned them the name "shot-hole borers". Bark beetles excavate tunnels beneath the bark and lay their eggs in them, and the young larvae excavate additional tunnels that radiate away from the first one. We find these galleries, many with symmetrical designs, by peeling off the loosened bark. The larvae develop within these tunnels and then as adults disperse to other dead trees. Once in a tree, the adults produce pheromones or sex attractants that bring additional bark beetles. They reproduce, forming large populations, and help break down the wood. These beetles are an important food for other animals, especially woodpeckers.

There are also larger wood-boring beetles, of both the metallic and long-horned types. The latter beetles may be two centimetres long. They have very long antennae and are sometimes brightly coloured. The larvae of these beetles make loud, rhythmic chewing noises with their impressive jaws; hence the name "sawyers".

A dead tree attracts many animals. Woodpeckers drum on dead wood and excavate their nesting cavities in it. In winter, these cavities are homes to flying squirrels, mice, woodpeckers, nuthatches and chickadees. Bats roost behind loose bark, tree swallows nest in holes, barred owls nest in hollow trunks, raccoons den under the roots and in large cavities, and hawks and eagles scan the countryside from the upper branches. Dead trees and trees with cavities are of crucial importance to forest wildlife.

Many different groups of living things become associated with a dead tree after it falls. Bacteria and fungi spread through the log and speed the natural decomposition process. Plants grow on decaying wood, and insects, salmanders, mice and shrews live in

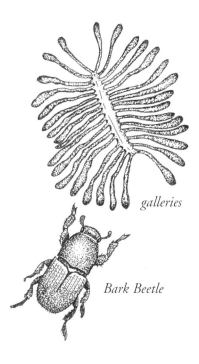

galleries

Bark Beetle

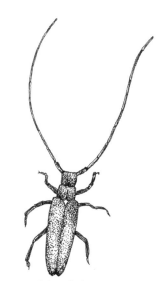

Round-headed Borer

and under rotting logs. A dead tree is full of life, and composting wood is essential to sustain the nutrient cycle and the diversity of woodland plants and animals.

Fallen trees and leaves cover the ground with a thick layer of litter. Plants and animals reduce this litter to humus, a partially decomposed organic material that improves the fertility and moisture retention of the soil. In turn, other organisms further digest the humus to add nutrients to the soil.

An enormous number of plants and animals live in litter, humus and the top few centimetres of the soil, and a search for them gives a good introduction to the complexities of litter decomposition and soil formation. Some animals chew up the fresh litter and break it into small fragments, and other animals feed on these fragments and digest them into their component proteins and carbohydrates. These animals include earthworms, a variety of beetles, mites, springtails, millipedes, centipedes, ants, snails and slugs. Many of these animals are small and a hand lens is needed to examine them.

Earthworms chew the leaves on the surface and pull them down into their burrows. They also ingest soil and digest its organic materials. Earthworms are important in the processes of fragmenting plant remains and mixing nutrients through the soil. They also have a role in aeration of the soil. In dry weather, earthworms can burrow to a depth of a metre or more to escape dehydration.

Mites and springtails also chew dead wood, leaves and large fungi and convert them into small fragments. Mites are oval with four pairs of legs. Some are colourless and others are black, dark brown or red. Although small, only one millimetre or less in length, they are present in large numbers and collectively are important agents in the decomposition process. Springtails are also numerous. They are wingless insects, about three millimetres in size, and have a "leaping" or "springing" organ. This rod-like structure extends forward from the underside of the abdomen. When this organ snaps down against the ground, it vaults the springtail several centimetres into the air. Looking for small, jumping "specks" is the easiest way to find them.

Under a Hand Lens

Springtail

Under a Microscope

Large numbers of microscopic plants and animals also live in the thin film of water that coats the soil particles. They may be seen by placing a little soil in a drop of water and examining it under a microscope. Bacteria, actinomycetes, fungi and protozoans all help build a nutrient-rich soil.

Bacteria are abundant, some rod-shaped and others spherical, and they join together to form chains. Some types of bacteria decompose litter and others concentrate phosphorus in the soil. Certain bacteria are "fixers" of nitrogen. That is, they convert atmospheric nitrogen into organic nitrogen compounds that can be used by plants and, in turn, by animals. To survive dry periods, some bacteria form spores and others enter a prolonged "stationary phase", a state that is similar to dormancy in other organisms.

Actinomycetes are formed by bacteria sticking together to form long, branching filaments. They resemble filamentous fungi and the name comes from Greek words that mean "fungus rays". In the soil, actinomycetes decompose plant material and the "earthy" odour of rich soil is partly caused by their secretions. Some actinomycetes, like certain bacteria, make atmospheric nitrogen available to plants. Plants, and animals in turn, obtain the nitrogen needed to synthesize protein from the activities of these bacteria and actinomycetes.

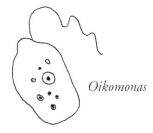

Oikomonas

Fungi appear as whitish threads, or hyphae, that run through the soil and rotting wood. The threads may be a few centimetres or up to a metre in length, and the larger ones can be seen without a microscope. Mushrooms, commonly seen above ground about decomposing litter, are the fruiting bodies or reproductive structures of these fungi. Fungi actively decompose litter and are among the few organisms that can digest both lignin and cellulose, two highly stable components of plant fibres.

Enormous numbers of protozoans live in soil water. They are single-cell organisms, but are easily seen under a microscope. *Colpoda* and *Oikomonas* are two types often present. *Colpoda* is oval and covered with beating cilia that propel it rapidly through the water. *Oikomonas* is also oval, with a rounded front end, and swims quickly by the lashing movements of its long, whip-like "tail" or flagellum. The protozoans feed on bacteria and fungi, and help control the growth of these populations.

Soil Organisms

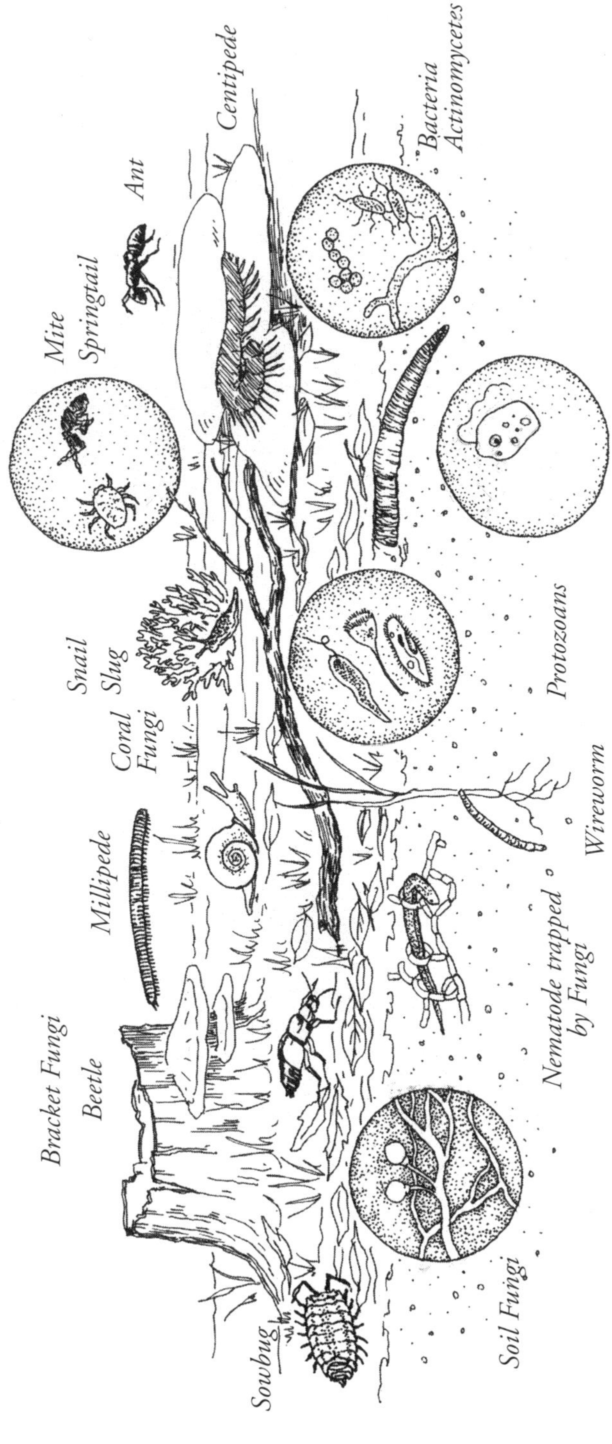

Bracket Fungi
Beetle
Millipede
Snail
Slug
Coral Fungi
Mite
Springtail
Ant
Centipede
Bacteria
Actinomycetes
Protozoans
Wireworm
Nematode trapped by Fungi
Sowbug
Soil Fungi

Tiny organisms such as these decompose litter and form a nutrient-rich soil. Soon new plants germinate, the nutrients are reused and the cycle is renewed. Nutrients circulate continuously between soil, plants and animals. This soil-plant-animal nutrient cycle is at the base of all terrestrial and aquatic communities. Sustaining this cycle must be the first consideration when caring for a wooded area. Ignoring this cycle quickly reduces the ability of the woodland to produce new growth.

*A Sense of
the Grand*

The tree species that grew here when the settlers arrived still grow in this area, but the giant trees of earlier times are almost all gone. Relicts can still be found and illustrate what the earlier forests were like. Several large yellow birches, 250 to 300 years old and a metre in diameter, are scattered along the mountain and giant hemlocks survive in deep ravines where cutting is not practical. Trees such as these once grew beside the tidal marsh where The Old Place now stands.

It is unfortunate that these magnificent forests were all cut and burned or destroyed by disease. Many years ago we worked in a forest of giant hemlocks (that has since been "harvested"). The lower limbs had fallen off and we could walk easily and quietly in all directions and gaze in wonder through the branches towering into the sky. People would better appreciate woodlands if they could walk among old trees that so delight the sense of the grand.

*Community
Woodland*

Can your community conserve a woodlot? Many people will enjoy the displays of wildflowers, searching for birds and mammals, and watching the activities of other living things. They will gain an understanding of the close relationships that exist between plants and animals, and realize that all these organisms are required to sustain a healthy woodland. A wooded area is full of inviting discoveries.

WOODLAND FLOWERS AND LICHENS

Like cultivated plants, the healthy growth of woodland flowers requires the appropriate amounts of light, water and minerals, and is enhanced by associations with fungi and a variety of soil organisms. Cutting and clearing wooded areas alter light and moisture levels. Also critical, but less evident, are the effects of changes in light and water plus chemical contamination on underground plant structures, root fungi and soil organisms. Conservation of areas in the "wild" state is an essential part of woodland planning, for both private and community sites.

Searching for wildflowers along the woodland path and watching them grow, blossom and produce seeds is an ongoing source of pleasure. Such observations reveal a variety of associations and specializations that enhances the growth of these plants. They also show that these plants require undisturbed conditions for growth, conditions that must be maintained if wildflowers are to survive in private and community woodlands.

Spring Flowers

The Mayflower is one of the earliest woodland plants to blossom each spring. We planted several under a red spruce after rescuing them from the side of a wood road that was being widened. They begin flowering in April and continue through much of May. Their flowers grow in clusters and are waxy and very fragrant. Most blossoms are white or pink, but some are dark and almost rose coloured. Mayflowers remain green all winter and the mats of green leaves, sometimes leathery and rusty, between patches of melting snow are welcome signs of approaching spring.

Pockets of mayflowers still grow in open deciduous and mixed woods on the mountain behind the village, but they are not as plentiful as they were only a decade ago. Like many woodland plants, mayflowers do not survive the habitat changes that often accompany lumbering and land development. Although once plentiful, mayflowers have all but disappeared from some areas of eastern North America. We can avoid the same loss here, but a special effort is needed to protect their habitat.

Woodland Flowers

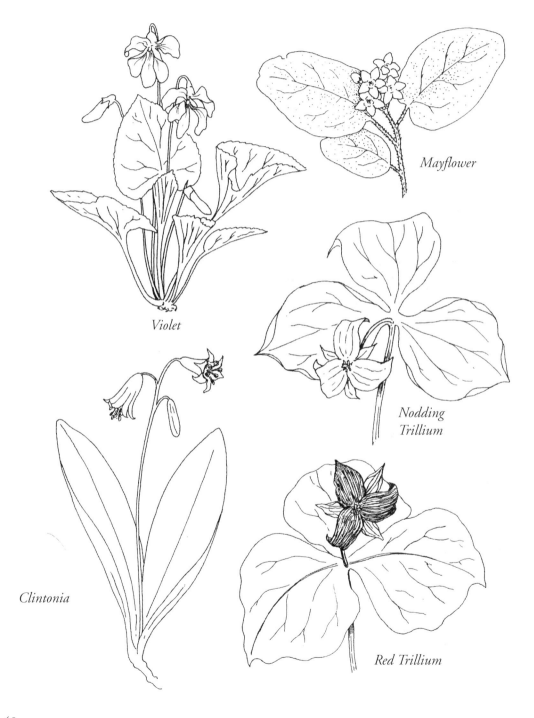

Violet

Mayflower

Nodding
Trillium

Clintonia

Red Trillium

We find the first violets in mid May, some blue and others white. Their delicate flowers confirm the arrival of spring. The northern blue violet is an early species to blossom. It grows near the pine trees. Its leaves are heart-shaped and both flowers and leaves are of the same height. This contrasts with the marsh blue violet, which grows on the meadow, and has flower stems that are taller than the leaf stems. Lance-leafed violet, with white flowers and elongate leaves, grows along the marshy border between the woodland and the meadow; and the small white violet, the smallest of the group with heart-shaped leaves, grows on the meadow. Other violets grow in the area, but these are the only ones that we have found at The Old Place with the exception, of course, of the cultivated pansies and Johnny-jump-ups.

A number of woodland plants flower in late May, some grow here naturally and we transplanted others to the property. Plants should not be taken from wild sites, unless disturbance of the sites threatens their survival. We planted a small bed of yellow clintonia among the spruce trees, having obtained them from a woodlot that was being cut to extend a farm field. Several wild lilies-of-the-valley were among the clintonia and both species are now spreading under the spruces. Clintonia produces clusters of yellowish, bell-shaped flowers. The leaves, like other lilies, are long and wide and have parallel veins. The leaves ensheath the base of the plant and then open to partially envelop the flower stalk. Yellow clintonia is also called the blue-bead lily because its round berries, which ripen in late summer, are dark blue.

Underground Stems

Many woodland plants reproduce vegetatively by means of rhizomes as well as by seeds. Rhizomes are underground stems and new plants grow from buds on these stems. All ferns have rhizomes and so does bunchberry, our smallest dogwood. The rhizomes of Dutchman's-breeches grow profusely and give rise to large clusters of plants. Rhizomes may live for a long time and produce a new growth of plants each year. Alternatively, the rhizomes of some species, like clintonia, live for only one year and then decay. Decay, however, frees the attached tubers and each produces a new plant that forms another rhizome to continue the cycle.

Ant Transport

Carex communis

Trilliums grow along the path and show the characteristic whorls of three broad leaves and flowers with three petals and three sepals. Wake-robin is another name for trillium. It is a favourite name because springtime walks to see the first flowers and returning birds are often associated with flowering trilliums. The flowers are striking, those of red trillium stand erect while those of nodding trillium hang below the leaves. The seeds ripen in August and, curiously, trilliums depend on ants to disperse them. Each seed is coated with a substance that attracts ants. The ants may carry a seed for several metres before eating this coating and dropping the seed, which then grows into a new plant. It takes several years for a new trillium to grow from seed and produce a flower.

Ants assist many woodland plants in seed dispersal. The tall fruit stalk of clintonia falls over when the berries are ripe and liberates its seeds onto the ground. Some seeds germinate beside the parent plant. Others are carried away by ants which are attracted by the tasty seed covering. Similarly, ants assist the woodland sedges in seed dispersal. Again, the tall stems bend to the ground when the seeds ripen and many seeds develop where they fall. This is one reason why sedges often grow in loose clumps, a habit described by the species name of one of our most common woodland sedges, *Carex communis*, where *communis* means "growing in colonies". In addition, a small bulb grows on the wall of the fruit as the seed develops. This bulb is packed with starch. The ants eat this starch and may carry the seeds several metres from the parent plant before dropping them.

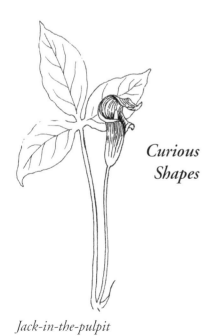

Jack-in-the-pulpit

Curious Shapes

Jack-in-the-pulpit is a curiously shaped plant, with small flowers clustered on a spike that stands inside a large, leafy bract. It has one or two leaves, each with a long stalk and divided into three leaflets. There are several plants near the beginning of the woodland path. While they do not flower until early June, we start looking for them in early May when the green and purplish shoots push up through the leaf litter. Unlike many plants which have both male and female parts in each flower, Jack-in-the-pulpit has flowers that are either male or female. Often the older plants are female and the younger ones are males, although an individual plant may change sex from year to year, a scheme to ensure successful reproduction. Female flowers are more numerous in years, following good growing seasons, when the plant has sufficient stored nutrients to enable the fruit to form and mature. Male flowers are more common in years when nutrient storage is low, and die after releasing their pollen. Female and male plants can sometimes be distinguished by the number of leaves. Plants with two leaves often have female flowers, and those with one leaf either have male flowers or do not form flowers. Attractive scarlet berries are present in autumn.

Pink Lady's-slipper

One woodland flower that we look for in early June is the pink lady's-slipper or moccasin flower. There are only a few plants along the woodland path, but their flowering signals the time for a walk on the mountain to a grove of pines where there are a few hundred of them. The single flower is distinctive, for its petals form a large pink pouch that hangs against a backing of green and brown sepals. Bees must crawl up through this pouch to collect nectar, and they pollinate the flower at the same time. Lady's-slippers are orchids and, like all orchids, must become associated with a fungus at an early stage of growth. The fungus absorbs water and minerals from the soil for use by the lady's-slipper and, in return, receives organic nutrients produced by the orchid. It takes several years for a seed to develop, become associated with a fungus, grow into a new plant and produce a flower. It takes only a second to pick and destroy it!

Summary Plants

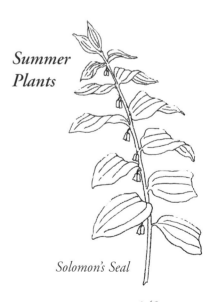

In summer, the tree leaves form a dense canopy and fewer woodland plants flower in the shade, although some plants of late spring continue to flower into early summer. Solomon's-seal flowers at this time. There is a bed of Solomon's-seal at the beginning of the woodland path growing under a maple tree. Each plant has a long wand-like stem, and the creamy flowers hang from the leaf axils along the length of the stem. Like other lilies, the flowers are bell-shaped. Blue berries form by early autumn and also hang from the leaf axils.

When walking on the mountain, it is easy initially to confuse Solomon's-seal, false Solomon's-seal and rose twisted-stalk, for all three have long, wand-like stems. However, the stems of rose

Solomon's Seal

twisted-stalk are zigzagged, and its flowers are rose coloured and hang along the stems on, as the name suggests, twisted stalks. In late summer, its berries are red, not blue. The flowers of false Solomon's-seal are creamy white and clustered at the end of the stems, and its fruit is white with brown speckles when first formed and later becomes ruby red.

Fungus-roots

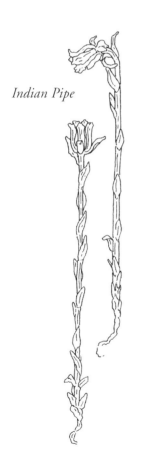

Indian Pipe

Scattered through the woods in mid and late summer is a plant that is all white, although it turns brown or black when it dies or is picked. Indian pipe is unique in that it lacks chlorophyll and is unable to carry on photosynthesis. Its stems are up to twenty centimetres high and its leaves are scale-like. It has a single, hanging flower, although the flower becomes erect after the seeds have formed. Indian pipe has an extensive root system that grows in association with mycorrhizae, a word that means "fungus-roots". This plant grows on decaying vegetable matter and also in close association with the mycorrhizae of trees, often coniferous trees. Like the fungus-entwined roots of lady's-slippers, the mycorrhizal filaments are highly efficient in absorbing water and minerals, especially phosphorus, from the soil for use by the tree. In return, the fungus obtains sugars and other organic nutrients manufactured by the tree. The mycorrhizae also conduct some of these nutrients and minerals to the Indian pipe. It is a three-way association: the coniferous tree, the Indian pipe and the mycorrhizae. The Indian pipe depends on the mycorrhizae for its nourishment, but its contribution to the association is not known.

Most wild and cultivated flowering plants, perhaps all, may grow in association with mycorrhizae, and the type of fungus is often specific for each plant. Some plants, like orchids and Indian pipes, require mycorrhizae for growth. Many plants can grow without mycorrhizae, but the fungus greatly enhances their growth. Not only do the fungi absorb water and minerals, they also act as a system of filters to protect the plant from toxic metals in the soil. Mycorrhizae enable plants to grow in habitats where conditions are less than optimal and, most importantly, they promote the recolonization of disturbed areas. It is this mycorrhizally-enhanced growth that enables beds of woodland plants, like teaberry and partridgeberry, to expand into the open and dry areas along roads and clearings.

Sometimes we see clusters of colourful scarlet "caps" when walking along the woodland path in late autumn and early winter before the snow is deep. These are British soldiers and are usually intermingled with pixie cups. Both are lichens that grow on rotting wood and poor soil. They are gray and about two centimetres high. The stems of British soldiers are branched and each branch has a scarlet cap. Pixie cups look like miniature wine glasses or goblets.

A lichen consists of a fungus and an alga living in partnership. The fungus encloses and protects the alga and, like a sponge, absorbs and holds the water needed by the alga to survive. The alga, through photosynthesis, produces the food needed by the fungus.

The scarlet caps of British soldiers are fruiting bodies and produce spores. Each spore grows into a fungal thread that must capture an alga, to provide its nourishment, if it is to survive. If successful, the two develop into a new lichen. Lichens, however, can also reproduce more simply. Small fragments break off and can grow into new lichens provided they contain both fungal and algal components and find appropriate conditions for growth.

Lichens have different shapes and many contain bright pigments. They decorate the rocks and trees with colourful patterns. There are several groups of lichens, based on shape. Wall lichens form flat, rosette-shaped encrustations on rocks and wood. They are orange or yellow-green, and sometimes are brightly coloured. Shield lichens resemble clusters of gray to yellowish or greenish leaves, and often grow on tree trunks. British soldiers and pixie cups grow upright on the ground and old wood, and old man's beard (p. 153) forms thick tangles of greenish strings that hang from trees. All groups are present along the woodland path.

Lichens can endure a wide range of temperatures and moisture conditions, and grow in most types of terrestrial environments. They are one of the primary manufacturers of soil. Lichens slowly dissolve and crumble rock and wood, and through their metabolic activities add the organic material needed to produce a film of soil. As the soil deepens, mosses start to grow and add more organic material and, gradually, the soil becomes deep enough to support other plants.

Lichens

British Soldiers

Pixie Cups

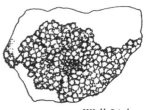

Wall Lichen

Shield Lichen

Today, researchers monitor the growth of lichens with interest, for it is a means of assessing air pollution. Lichens obtain the minerals required for metabolism from airborne moisture and dust. This makes them vulnerable to sulfur dioxide and other aerial poisons that interfere with the processes of photosynthesis in the algae. Death of lichens indicates that the quality of the air is deteriorating. The return of lichens, on the other hand, indicates an improvement in air quality.

Community Places for Peace and Enjoyment

Conservation of wooded areas in the natural state must be a part of community planning and private woodlot management. Natural sites best provide the specific physical, chemical and biological conditions needed for the healthy growth of plants and animals. Wooded areas are important to the quality of community life. They are quiet places where the richness and beauty of living things can be found and enjoyed.

BIRDING THE WOODLAND PATH

Several layers of vegetation and a supply of dead wood are required to make a wood-lot attractive to birds. Some birds dwell on the ground and others inhabit low shrubbery, prefer mid-sized trees or live in the canopy, and a few nest in the shrubbery and forage in the canopy. Many birds feed on the insects associated with dead wood, some nest in cavities excavated in softened wood, and others seek the shelter of such cavities in winter. Cutting all tall trees, removing dead and dying wood, and clearing out underbrush are common practices that seriously reduce the value of a woodlot for birds and other wildlife.

Many birds live or visit along the woodland path. Black-capped chickadees and white-breasted nuthatches are always there, brown creepers scamper around tree trunks in winter, and occasionally grosbeaks and crossbills forage in the ash and coniferous trees. Woodpeckers begin drumming in early spring and later thrushes and waves of warblers arrive, some for a short visit and others to stay for the summer. Early summer is a slow period with just a few thrushes, vireos and redstarts, but the woodland path provides the best birding of the year in late summer and fall when the post-nesting wanderers and migrants visit.

Small flocks of a dozen or fewer white-winged crossbills visit in most years. They are nomadic birds and wander widely in search of food. Crossbills feed on many types of seeds and fruit, but prefer the seeds of conifers and alders and travel great distances to find a good supply of cones. Their crossed bill is an adaptation to help pry the cones open. Crossbills do not breed when food is scarce, but may nest at any time of the year when food is plentiful. There is an open area of tall spruce and pine trees on the mountain where they nest. Their summer nest is a shallow cup of twigs and mosses. Their winter nest is heavily insulated with plant down and feathers and placed within a thick, supportive cluster of twigs at the end of a branch. The female must remain on the nest in winter to keep the eggs warm, and the male feeds her by regur-

Crossbills

White-winged Crossbill

gitating seeds into her throat. The males are in full song during nesting, and the trills and warbles are a joy to hear when we are skiing on the mountain.

Woodpeckers

Pileated Woodpecker

Downy Woodpecker

Downy woodpeckers and northern flickers nest at The Old Place. Hairy woodpeckers are frequent visitors, especially at winter feeders, and yellow-bellied sapsuckers visit during fall migration. Pileated woodpeckers come down from the mountain in late August to feed on the berries of the alternate-leafed dogwoods, and again in October when they swing about the vines of Virginia creeper to eat its berries. Both berries are among their favourites. In October 1992, a red-bellied woodpecker arrived and remained about the property and feeders until May. The frequent calls of this unusual visitor sounded like a flicker with a sore throat.

Downy woodpeckers are year-round residents and are frequent visitors to the suet feeder in the pine tree outside the kitchen window. They are our smallest woodpeckers. Both males and females are black and white and the males have a red patch on the back of their heads. Like other woodpeckers, downies have a "roller-coaster" flight pattern, and this plus their small size helps identify them as they fly across the lawn.

The downy woodpeckers nest in the old poplar trees and, like many woodpeckers, excavate their nest cavities in dead and slightly rotted wood. This emphasizes the importance of leaving dead trees and stumps standing. Downies also drum on dead wood, because the hard shell over a softened interior has excellent resonant properties. They begin excavating their nest cavity in late April, and may start several cavities before finishing one. The eggs are laid in late May and the young are about the garden in early July. Downies also use these cavities for shelter in winter, or chisel out new ones. Other winter birds, such as chickadees and nuthatches, crowd together for mutual warmth in unused woodpecker cavities.

Downies feed primarily on insects and search through the shrubs and trees to find them. They also eat berries in summer and visit our suet feeders in winter. Downies consume large numbers of corn borers and are an important means of naturally controlling this agricultural pest. When we ski across farm fields, we usually see one or two pairs working through the corn stubble.

A pair of flickers also nests at The Old Place. We are first aware of their return each spring when we hear their loud, resonant drumming and repeated "wicker-wicker-wicker" calls, and soon we see them flying across the lawn and meadow. Presumably, this is the same pair that nested here in previous years. Their undulating flight pattern, yellow under-wings and conspicuous white rumps make their identification an easy one.

The flickers begin excavating a new nesting hole in an old poplar or elm tree in early May, although there may be several holes already in the trunk from previous years. We placed a nesting box in a tree nearby, but they prefer to construct their own cavity and have never used it. Both the male, recognized by his black moustache, and female take part in excavating the cavity and later share the task of incubating the eggs and feeding the young. The eggs are laid in mid May and about three weeks later we see five or six young looking out of the hole. They leave the cavity after another week, but remain about the property while they learn the techniques of foraging from their parents.

Yellow-shafted Flicker

Flickers eat insects of all types and catch them both on the ground and during flight. Ants are their primary summer food, and flickers often feed on the path or driveway where they pick them up with their tongue. Their tongue is almost four centimetres long, and the end is covered with bristles and coated with a sticky saliva. In late summer, they also feast on the grasshoppers that are so abundant on the meadow, and in autumn they add berries to their menu.

In seasons when there is little snow, flickers may remain in the area until Christmas and a few stay all winter. At these times, we find them in small groups, presumably family groups, in old fields where there is an abundance of bayberries. They also visit our bird feeders and have a preference for cracked corn. However, most flickers migrate south in September and October. Locally, they follow the mountain range during migration, and at peak periods in late September it is not unusual to have forty or more flickers about The Old Place.

Vireos

Listening to the red-eyed vireos is one of the pleasures of a woodland walk in late spring and early summer. Only the male sings. He returns first, in late May, and begins singing immediately and continues singing throughout the nesting period. His notes are clearly heard, but it is often difficult to locate the singer for he forages in the canopy of the tall elm and oak trees, where he acrobatically flits about the twigs and leaves looking for insects. He allows only quick glimpses, hardly long enough to focus the binoculars for a good view.

However, we start hunting when he stops singing for we know from previous watching that he then drops down to the lower branches and shrubbery, perhaps to bring food to the nesting female. The female inhabits the understory and it is at such times that we get the best views of the two of them. Their plumages are the same. Both are olive above, white below and have blue-gray crowns. A white line, outlined with black, above the eye is the best identifying feature. The red eye is present only in adult birds.

Red-eyed Vireo

We find their nest in most years, often in the same shadbush and suspended from a forked branch about three metres above the ground. It is made of strips of bark and lined with fine grasses and plant down. Often the bark of white birch is used for there are two birch trees nearby. The three, sometimes four, eggs take about two weeks to hatch and both parents feed the young. The vireos leave in September for their wintering areas in South America.

Regretfully, populations of red-eyed vireos are in decline. These birds require thick undergrowth for nesting and tall trees for foraging. The expansion of forestry, agriculture and communities reduces the availability of this habitat.

Warblers

On early morning walks through mid August, and with a little luck, the list of birds seen along the woodland path is a "Who's Who" of Nova Scotian warblers. Black-and-white, Tennessee, Nashville, northern parula, yellow, magnolia, black-throated blue, yellow-rumped, black-throated green, blackburnian, chestnut-sided, bay-breasted, blackpoll, mourning, common yellowthroat, Canada, palm, and American redstart have all been

Woodland Warblers

Blackpoll

Black and White

Black-throated Blue

Bau-breasted

Magnolia

Chestnut-sided

Canada

sighted along the walk, many on a regular basis. A friend sometimes joins me on an August morning and we list and count the
warblers. To date, our warbler record for one pre-breakfast walk is:
12 species, 65 individuals, and species highs of 20 yellow and 15
Tennessee warblers.

Four or five blackpoll and one or two bay-breasted warblers visit the property during the second half of May. They stay
for a few days and then leave to nest elsewhere. In spring, the
chestnut colouring of the bay-breasted is striking and easily dis-
tinguishes it from the blackpoll with its gray and black stripes and
solid black cap. However, both species return in August and we see
them regularly from then through much of September. The two
are difficult to identify in autumn. Both are olive green with two
white wing-bars; but the bay-breasted is buff-coloured under its
tail and has dark legs, while the under-tail of the blackpoll is white
and most have yellowish legs. Although it takes practice and
patience to distinguish these two species in autumn, their visits are
especially welcomed when we recall that their stay is just one stop
on their long migration route. The bay-breasted likely remained in
this area to nest; but the blackpoll may have flown much further
north, some to the limits of the tree line. Their winter homes are
in South America, those of the bay-breasted in Venezuela and
those of the blackpoll between Venezuela and central Chile. The
extremes of the blackpoll's range make it the champion long-dis-
tance flier among the songbirds.

In early June each year, we plan a walk on the mountain
to look for warblers and to enjoy the spring flowers. At this time,
spring-beauties and Dutchman's-breeches carpet the deciduous
woods, there are large patches of white and blue violets, and red
trilliums are just beginning to open. We find black-throated blue
warblers there, in an open area of tall beech and red maple trees.
The area has a heavy undergrowth of alders, viburnums, laurels
and dense thickets of young balsam fir. This is the habitat that
these birds prefer, one in which they can forage for insects in the
tops of trees and nest in the dense understory. Black-throated
blues wander more widely after nesting and it is then that they
come to The Old Place. The male, strikingly coloured with a blue-
gray back, white underparts and black sides and face, is easily rec-

ognized. The females and young, however, are olive coloured and difficult to identify until we see the small white patch on the edge of the wing. They leave in late September to winter in southern Florida and the West Indies.

Each spring we also look for northern parulas on the mountain, and watch them search, "chickadee-style", over the ends of hemlock and spruce branches for insects. There is one place where they are always present. It is an open stand of red maple and the branches are heavily draped with old man's beard, a lichen formed of hanging gray-green strings. We found this spot by accident. While stopping for an afternoon rest and coffee during a birding trip, we saw a parula fly into a clump of old man's beard on a branch about four metres away. The parula quickly flew off but returned in a few moments, and continued to fly to and from that clump of lichen. It was mid June and we realized that we had found a nest, for locally parulas nest only in thick masses of old man's beard.

Parulas come to The Old Place in August after nesting, and we often see one or two during morning walks from then until mid October. Stragglers continue to visit at later dates and we have found them as late as December 16. The late stragglers are the most conspicuous, perhaps because the leaves have fallen and the other warblers but for a few yellow-rumps have left. At these times, the parula's unique blue and green back, yellow breast with necklace, and white eye-ring clearly stand out in the morning sun against the evergreen boughs and brown branches of the deciduous trees. Winter begins when the parulas leave.

To provide food and nesting sites and to be attractive to birds, a woodlot must have areas of thick ground-cover and several strata of shrubs and trees, including tall trees. Dead trees are important as sources of food, nesting cavities and winter shelters. Natural woodlands provide all these requirements and must be conserved if we are to keep a variety of woodland birds about our communities.

Parula Warbler in
Old Man's Beard Lichen

Natural
Habitats
Required

WOODLAND MARSH

Wetlands are among our most valuable ecosystems. They ensure improved water quality both underground and downstream. Wetlands hold water and reduce flooding, and release water over time to replenish the flow in streams and rivers. The extensive growth of plants in wetlands reduces erosion, and builds a rich soil that helps maintain the high productivity of the system. A great variety of plants and animals live in association with wetlands and many are dependent upon them for successful reproduction. A special effort is now needed to maintain and restore these ecosystems, and the plants and animals that are a part of them.

Trees and Shrubs

Box-elder

The end of the woodland path curves down to the northwest corner of the meadow. A few decades ago this area was a freshwater marsh, but it had been ditched and partially drained. We closed the ditch and allowed the marsh to restore itself and now, although small, it supports a wealth of plants and animals.

Behind the marsh, there is a bank that slopes up to the highway. The bank partially encircles the marsh, like an amphitheatre. Elm and ash trees grow on it naturally, and we added spruce trees to block off the sights and sounds of the highway and box-elders for a supply of winter food. The morning sun shines into this amphitheatre first, and with its warmth the trees become alive with birds.

Box-elder, or Manitoba maple, is a small tree and one that grows quickly. It is a type of maple but, unlike other local maples, each leaf is divided into three or more leaflets. In this respect, the leaves resemble those of ash and the tree is sometimes called ash maple. However, its seeds are paired and have two wings as do all maples, while those of ashes are single with only one wing. Also, the seeds of box-elder, unlike other maples, remain on the trees into winter. Evening and pine grosbeaks and cedar and Bohemian waxwings feast on these seeds.

We wanted a border of tall shrubs to create an intermedi-

154

ate level between the trees on the bank and the floor of the marsh. This layer is used by those birds that live in the lower strata but require more shelter than is available on the meadow. Also, we wanted a variety of shrubs to give a succession of food through the seasons. At the edge of the marsh there are two old, twisted honeysuckles. These form the centre of the stratum, we allowed buckthorn and wild roses to grow with them, and we planted red-berried elder and highbush cranberry. Thus, one side of the marsh is bordered by a bank covered with trees and the opposite side, along the meadow, by dense thickets.

The showy blossoms of red-berried elder appear in late May and early June, about the same time as its leaves are unfolding. Each spray is oval-shaped and composed of many white flowers. The berries are red and ripen in July, and are devoured quickly by robins and waxwings. Common elder also grows in the marsh. Its sprays of white flowers are flat-topped and appear during the second half of July. The dark purple fruit matures in autumn and is also eaten by birds and other wildlife. The buds aid identification in winter. They are arranged in opposite pairs in both species: those of red-berried elder are large and oval, while those of common elder are small and conical. Checking the colour of the pith also helps distinguish these two shrubs: it is brown in red-berried elder and white in common elder. The pith is easily removed and the tube may be used to make whistles and flutes. The scientific name of elder is *Sambucus,* a Greek word for a type of harp made partly of elder wood. We hope that it was more musical than the whistles that we made when we were in school.

Red-berried Elder

Highbush cranberry is a type of viburnum and not a true cranberry, although the fruit resembles that of cranberry. It transplants easily and we planted several that we obtained from a farm woodlot where they grow profusely. Highbush cranberries are tall shrubs, with oppositely-arranged buds and leaves, and each leaf has three lobes. They produce showy clusters of white flowers during the second half of June and early July, and clusters of bright red berries in autumn that remain on the shrub over winter. The berries are most colourful against the winter snow. The leaves also turn brick red after the first frosts and add to the displays of autumn colours. Birds do not eat the fruit until late winter when

Highbush Cranberry

other sources of food are becoming scarce, and the cold has made it more palatable. Pine grosbeaks and waxwings feed on the fruit of highbush cranberry in late winter, and rose-breasted grosbeaks eat any remaining fruit when they return in spring.

The honeysuckles blossom in late May and early June, and their flowers and associated insects attract hummingbirds and a variety of warblers. The fruit ripens in early August, and thrushes, waxwings and grosbeaks quickly devour it. The rose hips also ripen in late summer, but the thickets are extensive and are not stripped until the large flocks of robins return in early spring.

Wild Flowers and Seeds

A large stand of fireweed borders the front of the marsh, where it continues into the meadow. Fireweed becomes conspicuous in early July when its long stems of pink buds rise above its purplish stalks and leaves. The buds start to open in mid July and continue to flower through August. The floral spires may reach two metres in height by late summer, and new buds form as they lengthen. Thus, in August, the upper portion of the spire is pink with young buds, the mid portion is pink to purple with mature flowers, and the lower portion is green to brown with curved seed pods from the first-formed flowers. The pods open in autumn and the seeds, each with a silky white tassel, blow away in the wind.

Arrow-leafed tearthumb starts to grow in early spring, but is most evident in late summer and autumn when it reaches up to two metres in length. It is a sprawling plant and forms dense networks through the grass. Tearthumb is a type of buckwheat and, like other buckwheats, its stems are four-sided, jointed, and have swollen nodes that are each enveloped by a sheath. Fine spines cover the stems and, because the nodes break easily, our clothing is covered with pieces of stem after a walk through the marsh; and our legs if not protected are thoroughly scratched. Scratch-grass, appropriately, is another name for tearthumb. Tearthumb blossoms from early August to October. The flowers are small, white and generally inconspicuous. However, they produce enormous numbers of seeds and song sparrows, white-throated sparrows, tree sparrows, juncos and goldfinches flit about the marsh feeding on them during late autumn and winter.

Fireweed

Cattails grow at one end of the marsh. They flower during May, June and July. The dense cylinder of pistillate or seed- producing flowers is the familiar one, but there is also a spike of staminate or pollen-producing flowers projecting above it. The wind disperses the pollen in yellowish puffs with each breeze. These upper flowers fall off after releasing their pollen, leaving a bare spike. The inflorescence is green when first formed, but turns brown after pollination. Many of the brown pistillate flowers fall apart during winter, and the wind also disperses their cotton-like clusters of seeds. The plants within the colony grow and spread primarily from underground rhizomes, while the seeds disperse to produce new plants in other locations.

A cattail marsh has been likened to a kidney. A kidney functions in filtering body fluids, conserving valuable materials for further use, and removing toxic substances. A cattail marsh filters water, builds rich soil to support further growth, and removes toxic substances. Cattails are perennials, with the upper parts dying back each winter and with new growth produced each spring. As the plants grow, they store an enormous amount of organic material and, with die-back, this material decays and helps build the rich soil of the marsh. Cattails, and other marsh plants such as bulrushes, possess chemical and biological mechanisms that capture toxic substances and remove them from the water. Some bacteria in the marsh soil oxidize and precipitate metals, and other bacteria reduce iron and sulphate compounds into less toxic substances. In addition, the removal of these harmful chemicals changes the pH of the water from an acidic to a more alkaline range. The result is that the water leaving a cattail marsh is of better quality than that entering it. Some communities now plant large cattail marshes as part of their water-treatment systems. Ecologically, a cattail marsh is valuable real estate.

The wet marsh and surrounding bushes provide an ideal habitat for spring peepers, and their choruses are one of the notable sounds of spring. They call mostly at night and, curiously, a naturalist friend, Sherman Williams, noted that they also started calling in the middle of the day during an eclipse of the sun that occurred on May 10, 1994. The full chorus begins in mid

Filtration System

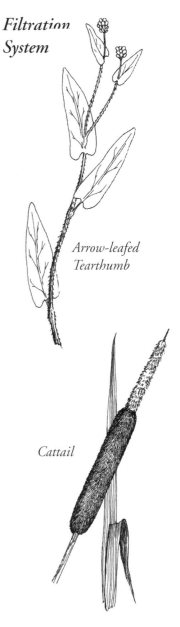

Arrow-leafed Tearthumb

Cattail

Amphibians

Frog Development

Egg

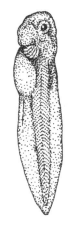

Hatching

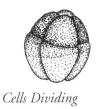

Cells Dividing

Folds Forming Brain

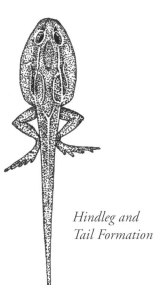

*Hindleg and
Tail Formation*

April and continues until the end of May. We look for peepers with a flashlight, for their vocal or throat sacs enlarge when thcy call and reflect the light. It is always surprising to find a spring peeper and realize that the frog with such a loud voice is only two or three centimetres long. The individual peeper is brown or tan and often has dark markings that may resemble a cross on its back. It is a type of tree frog and has adhesive pads on its toes that help it climb into bushes and trees. In summer, adult and young peepers migrate from the marsh into the woods and later overwinter there buried in the moss and leaf litter. They emerge again the following April and return to the marsh to begin another chorus.

Wood frogs are also present along the lower, wetter portions of the woodland path and, each spring, we hear their hoarse, clacking notes mixed with the calls of the spring peepers. Also, we find the jelly clumps of their egg masses in the water. The clumps are spherical and not flattened like the egg-rafts of green frogs. However, we rarely see a wood frog for they live on land and hide in the moss and leaf litter. They are easily recognized when seen for they have a black mask that extends from the nose through the eyes and ear drums. The scientific name of the wood frog is an appropriate one, for *sylvatica* means "growing among trees".

Spring peepers, wood frogs, leopard frogs and toads lay eggs in spring. The rate of development depends on water temperature, but tiny tadpoles may hatch in five days and grow into small frogs by mid summer. Green frogs, on the other hand, do not lay their eggs until mid summer. Their tadpoles overwinter and transform into froglets the following spring.

The upper half of each egg contains brown pigment, while the lower half is full of yolk and is white or yellowish. A protective layer of jelly surrounds each egg. The egg divides into smaller cells within a few hours of laying. By two days and with a hand lens, we can see ridges along the upper surface of the embryo. These are the beginnings of the brain and spinal cord. The tail starts to develop at about four days, and by day five, again with a hand lens, the gills and pulsating movements in the throat are evident. These movements indicate that the heart has formed and started beating.

Wood Frog

Spring Peeper —
Throat Sac Enlarged

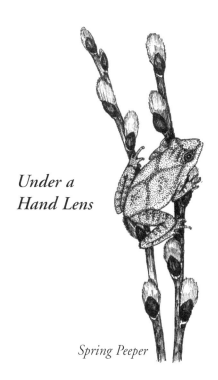

Under a
Hand Lens

Spring Peeper

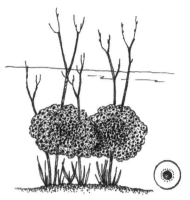

Wood Frog Egg Mass

Stewardship of Entire Ecosystems

After hatching, the tadpoles remain attached to submerged plants for a few days and feed by scraping algae off the stems and leaves. During this time, the tail grows deeper and the tadpole starts swimming. The tadpole continues to grow and, at about three months, it is a miniature frog. It also changes from feeding on plants to eating insects and other small animals during this period, and it stops using its gills and starts using its lungs. At first the young frog swims with its hind legs, which have been present in miniature since hatching. Later, the fore legs appear, usually the left one first, and finally the tail gradually shrinks and disappears.

Wetlands are continuously being destroyed by draining and filling, often by communities and land owners. The need to protect and restore them is an urgent one. Many conservation programmes are initiated by government and work down to the local level. It is also important to begin at the local level and expand to entire ecosystems. Individuals, groups of land owners, communities and groups of communities can work together to establish conservation programmes. There are excellent examples of such cooperative actions. Some conserve and restore entire water systems that, from headwaters to large rivers, extend many kilometres in length and border several communities. Forested areas and seashores can be protected in the same way. While these projects may require large organizations, they often originate through the efforts of a few concerned individuals.

WINTER WOODLAND

Winter is an excellent time to start watching nature. There are many plants and animals to search for, and the ways in which they survive the cold add interesting behaviours to observe. Winter survival requires food and shelter, and healthy woodlands best provide both requirements. However, food and shelter are steadily being lost as woodlands are cut. We must work to conserve wooded areas if we are to enjoy wild plants and animals about our homes and communities.

There is much to see during a walk along the woodland path in winter. Patches of evergreen plants stand out against the sere ground-cover and early snow, and thickets of shrubs provide food and shelter for birds and mammals. Identification of shrubs after the leaves have fallen is often a challenging task. There are fewer birds than in summer, but their numbers are sufficient to make the search a worthwhile one and the ways in which they cope with the cold are quite remarkable. Mammals are difficult to find at all times of the year, but tracks in the snow record their presence and show where and how they live.

Several plants remain green throughout winter and sometimes are gathered for use in making festive decorations. Tree clubmoss or ground pine and staghorn clubmoss are common species. Their trailing stems and upright branches have scale-like leaves, like true mosses, and their reproductive cones resemble clubs. These cones are usually at the tops of the branches and produce clouds of spores that form a yellowish dusting over the snow. Clubmosses are similar in miniature to the giant *Lepidodendron* trees that grew here 300 million years ago. At that time, the climate was warm and moist and supported a luxuriant growth of plant life.

The Christmas fern is another plant that remains green throughout winter. Its leaves droop and spread over the ground with the frosts of autumn, yet remain alive until the new fiddle-

Winter Greens

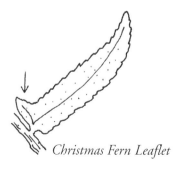

Christmas Fern Leaflet

Winter Greens

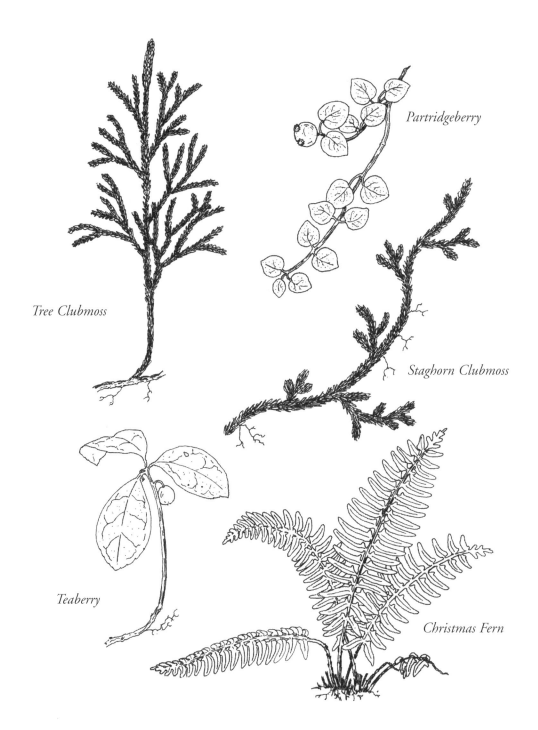

Tree Clubmoss

Partridgeberry

Staghorn Clubmoss

Teaberry

Christmas Fern

heads begin to uncurl in spring. The leaves form patches of green that show wherever the snow has melted during winter thaws. A small lobe at the base of each leaflet makes the identification of Christmas ferns an easy task. The lobe is sometimes described as a "toe" and the leaflet as "boot-shaped". Presumably, it is called Christmas fern because it is green at Christmas time and often used when decorating for the holiday season. Actually, it is used in flower arrangements throughout the year, and many gardeners cultivate it for this purpose.

Partridgeberry and teaberry are also evergreens and show through the shallow snows of early winter. Both are low plants and form broad carpets. Partridgeberry has oval, paired leaves, often with white veins, that are arranged along the length of the trailing stems. Those of teaberry are dark green, sometimes with a reddish tinge, leathery and shiny, and usually clustered at the ends of upright branches. In winter, both partridgeberry and teaberry have bright red berries that stand out against the green leaves and snow. The berries of partridgeberry are unique. In summer, the ovaries of its paired flowers fuse and, consequently, each berry is double and has two sets of seeds. The berries remain on both plants all winter, or until eaten by birds and other animals.

Wintergreen is another name for teaberry. Oil of wintergreen is one of its constituents and gives the leaves and berries a pleasant fragrance. A tea with a refreshing aroma may be brewed from this plant. In earlier times, settlers used this tea as a general tonic and to prevent scurvy. It was effective because, as is now known, the plant contains a high content of vitamin C. Extracts of this plant were also used to ease toothaches and headaches. Again they were effective because the plant contains salicylates which relieve pain. Some modern, commercial preparations to ease pain also contain salicylates.

A variety of shrubs form the woodland understory: bayberries, viburnums, buckthorns, witch-hazels and extensive tangles of wild roses. Bayberries have pleasantly aromatic leaves and twigs and are also used for their fragrance when decorating. The leaves stay green until late autumn. Some dried leaves remain on the shrub and aid identification in winter, after which the round-

Winter Shrubs

Bayberry

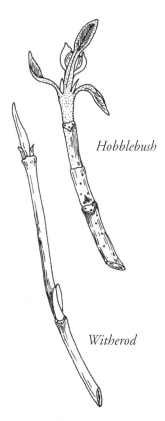

Hobblebush

Witherod

ed buds and upturned twigs are helpful clues.

The berries form conspicuous clusters by early autumn. They are dark blue and covered with a white wax. This wax can be boiled off and used to make candles that have a pleasant aroma. Hence, "candleberry shrub" is another name for bayberry. The berries would make this shrub easy to identify after its leaves have fallen, but they are quickly eaten by birds.

Not all bushes produce berries. The male and female flowers occur on separate shrubs, and one shrub may be laden with berries while the adjacent male shrub has none. Furthermore, influenced by adverse growing conditions, the female shrubs may change into male shrubs, and then revert to female when conditions for growth improve. Consequently, bushes that have not produced fruit for several years may one autumn be covered with clusters of berries.

The berries are favourites of yellow-rumped warblers, robins and flickers, and these birds congregate in large numbers in bayberry thickets during autumn and winter. The local race of the yellow-rumped warbler is the myrtle warbler, so called because of its preference for the berries of wax-myrtle, another name for bayberry. When berries survive the winter, they provide an emergency food for early spring migrants. Several years ago, the tree swallows arrived as usual in late April, but by early May the weather had turned cold with snow flurries and there were no flying insects. The tree swallows congregated in the shelter of a nearby ravine and fed on bayberries. This adaptability may explain why tree swallows overwinter further north, and arrive earlier in spring, than do the other species of swallows.

Two viburnum species, hobblebush and wild raisin or witherod, grow along the woodland path and produce showy clusters of white flowers in late spring and early summer. The clusters of flowers have outer blossoms that are large and white and inner blossoms that are less conspicuous. The outer blossoms are sterile, but they attract insects that pollinate the flowers in the centre. In autumn, clusters of blue berries cover both viburnums. Robins and waxwings eagerly seek these berries, as do squirrels and mice. The buds make identification of viburnums in winter an easy task. They are characteristically elongate and stalked, and arranged in opposite pairs. In late winter, the developing leaves give the buds a greenish colour.

Witch-hazel blooms in October and November. It is the last of our woodland shrubs and trees to flower and it continues to flower into early winter, by which time its leaves have fallen. For this reason, winterbloom is another common name for witch-hazel. The flowers are yellow and each has four long, ribbon-like petals. The fruiting capsules are greenish when young and take about two years to mature. When ripe, the capsules suddenly split and eject their nuts over a distance of several metres. The split capsules, brown and woody, remain on the shrub over winter and provide a good identification aid. Many birds and mammals eat the nuts.

Witch-hazel

Several species of birds visit the woodland in winter. Golden-crowned kinglets, red-breasted nuthatches and an occasional boreal chickadee forage in the coniferous trees, hairy and downy woodpeckers search for insects in the deciduous trees, and in some years we enjoy visits by pine grosbeaks.

Winter Birds

Pine grosbeaks travel widely in search of food, but a few flocks of six to ten birds visit briefly during most winters. Rarely, flocks of a few hundred birds arrive and stay for several days. They eat seeds and those of white ash are favourites. The male pine grosbeaks are bright rose-red, the females are olive and yellow, and when present in large numbers they trim the trees like Christmas decorations. February 1993 was such an occasion, when flocks totalling over 300 birds were present in the area. Such large flocks, while unusual today, occurred here more frequently 50 years and more ago. Possibly, the gradual warming of the climate is making this area less attractive to these northern birds.

The golden-crowned kinglets often visit in the company of red-breasted nuthatches and black-capped chickadees. They flit over the ends of the evergreen branches, sometimes hanging upside down, searching for insects, spiders and eggs. Their calls, uttered continuously, are contact notes that help keep the members of the flock together. Flocks of mixed species are common in winter. The larger number of birds improves their chances of finding good feeding sites, and species with different foraging habits

Pine Grosbeak

and dietary preferences are able to take full advantage of the better sites without competing with one another.

How do small birds survive cold temperatures? A supply of good quality food is required to maintain the high rate of metabolism needed to generate heat, for their small bodies have proportionally large surfaces through which heat may be lost. Heat conservation also requires shelter and good insulation. Chickadees forage throughout the day and have several feeding sites that they visit on a regular basis. They also store food for later use. Chickadees enter a shelter at night, such as a tree cavity, where several huddle together for mutual warmth. There they fluff-out their feathers to entrap layers of warm air and form a thick insulation. Like many winter birds, chickadees shiver to generate heat through muscle activity. They also become torpid at night. That is, they lower their heart rate, respiration rate and body temperature to save energy, and remain torpid until morning.

Kinglets behave differently from chickadees in response to cold. Kinglets do not cache food, roost in cavities or become torpid. Their body weight increases during the day while they are feeding and then drops at night as they use energy to generate heat by shivering. At night, several kinglets may huddle together within the shelter of a coniferous tree, as fluffy balls aligned on a branch.

Many winter birds have a type of fat that is different from the type used to store nourishment. It is similar to the heat-producing fat described for the meadow jumping mouse. Possibly, this tissue also produces heat in birds and provides the "quick heat" needed in emergencies and to arouse the bird from torpidity in the morning.

Black-capped Chickadee

Golden-crowned Kinglet

Winter Mammals

Squirrels are always fun to watch. A red squirrel is resident at The Old Place, a second one visits from time to time, and occasionally we see a northern flying squirrel. Unlike many mammals, red squirrels are active during the day, although they have a midday rest. Red squirrels usually live in tree cavities, wood piles or underground tunnels, but the one at The Old Place lives in the ice house. Its loud chatter is a familiar sound as it races through the trees, sometimes leaping several metres from one branch to the next. When disturbed, it sits up and scolds our intrusion, but if we wait quietly its curiosity wins and it comes down to have a better look at us.

Red Squirrel

Tracks show where the squirrel feeds and travels, although they are difficult to follow for they appear and disappear as the squirrel scampers up one tree and over the branches to another. There are four prints in the track: two large prints of the hind feet in front of the two small prints of the fore feet. Squirrels eat seeds and nuts of all kinds and may dig through the snow to search for them. The seeds of coniferous trees are favourites and mounds of cones and scales mark the sites where they feed. Our pile of fire wood is one such perch and is capped by a layer of cone fragments several centimetres deep. Squirrels also harvest cones and store them in underground caches for use when needed. A cache may contain several litres of cones and this makes squirrels valuable foresters, for some of the buried seeds germinate and grow into new trees. Red squirrels are fond of mushrooms, which they store in caches, and also enjoy sweets. They obtain sweets by chewing holes in the bark of sugar maples on warm days in late winter, and returning later to feast on the sugary sap that collects in the well.

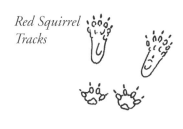
Red Squirrel Tracks

It is likely that northern flying squirrels are regular visitors to The Old Place, but they are active at night and are seen less frequently than red squirrels. We see one occasionally, often near midnight, eating sunflower seeds at the bird feeder on the window sill. It is fawn-coloured and has a round head with large eyes. Flying squirrels have a sheet of skin along their sides connecting the fore and hind legs. They do not actually fly, but glide for considerable distances by stretching this skin to make a wing and using their tails as rudders.

Flying squirrels glide from tree to tree and down to scamper about on the ground. Their tracks are the same as those of red squirrels, but begin with a "landing splash" in the snow. Flying squirrels live in cavities in trees during the day, and sometimes in attics and vacant buildings. They are likely the basis for many stories of haunted houses.

Deer mice are also common in the woodland. The adults are cinnamon in colour, with white underparts, and have a long tail and conspicuously large ears. The young are gray. Deer mice

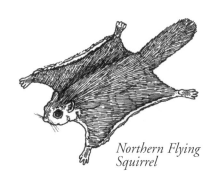
Northern Flying Squirrel

Deer Mouse

are nocturnal and seldom seen during a walk or ski, but their tracks record their presence. The tracks are easily found about brush piles and on logs that they use as runways. The tracks are small and show the drag marks of the long tails.

Deer mice feed chiefly on seeds. They are also fond of mushrooms, berries, nuts, insects and many small invertebrates. They store several litres of food for winter, and carry the food to their caches by stuffing it into their cheek pouches or by dragging berries and nuts with their front paws. At night deer mice visit the bird feeder on the window sill, and stamp their front feet to show their annoyance when we disturb them by turning on the light.

Community Inventory

Winter is an excellent time to start compiling an inventory of the wild plants and animals that live about your property or community. The task is one that generates an awareness and appreciation for natural sites, and for the diversity of living things. An inventory should include information such as species present, numbers, habitat, time of year and food sources. Naturalists participating in community planning require such documentation when preparing proposals to conserve natural places

HISTORIC GARDENS

"This is the forest primeval, the
murmuring pines and hemlocks."

Evangeline
H. W. Longfellow, 1847.

EARLY GARDENS

Climatic changes can dramatically alter plant and animal populations. This is illustrated by examining the natural history of our area during times when the climate was different. Population changes caused by natural agents are often difficult to distinguish from those caused by human activity. We cannot do anything about climatic change caused by such factors as galactic dust, continental movement, or shifts in ocean beds. However, we can limit change caused by such factors as atmospheric pollution, diversion of bodies of fresh water, and loss of vegetation covering. Can you and your community work to reduce the influences of human activity on climate?

Tundra Garden

The Palaeo-Indian people inhibited this region during the period following the glaciers. As the ice melted, they followed the animals north from the present area of New England. The Palaeo-Indian people established at least one settlement, dating about 10,600 years ago, near the north shore of the Minas Basin. From there, hunting and fishing parties crossed the Basin and visited the area of The Old Place, for projectile points characteristic of their culture were found on a farm only a few kilometres away.

At that time, the Minas Basin was much smaller than it is today, the present high tides were absent, and the expansive tidal marshes had not formed. While the continental glaciers had retreated, ice caps persisted on nearby hills and continued to influence the local climate. The annual temperature averaged 0°C and the ground was permanently frozen. The garden at that time grew under conditions similar to those now found on the tundra, and reference to present-day alpine and arctic plants and animals helps us reconstruct it.

The environment was a harsh one with a short growing season, drying winds, snow, and poor drainage caused by permafrost. The vegetation was typically low and often mat-like. Sedges and grasses made up much of the ground cover, mosses were abundant, and lichens formed thick carpets over the rocks and woody plants.

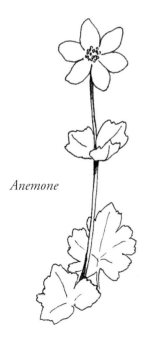

Anemone

The flowering plants, like sedums and saxifrages, were dwarf forms with rosettes of leaves placed near the ground to limit exposure and evaporation. These plants were dormant for most of the year and had short reproductive cycles. They grew, flowered and produced seeds during the short summer. In some species, the flower buds developed fully while covered with snow and then opened quickly when the snow melted. The blossoms were large and brightly coloured, and were quickly pollinated. Anemones, cinquefoils, buttercups, gentians, pinks and poppies were likely among the flowering plants that grew in the area of The Old Place during the Palaeo-Indian period.

Labrador Tea

Woody plants were also low, often creeping. Carpets of crowberry covered large areas of the ground, and shrubs like blueberry, bearberry, Labrador-tea, leatherleaf, alder and rhododendron were likely present. Trees, mainly birch and willow, were prostrate and even old trees grew to only a few centimetres in height. Their trunks were thick and twisted along the ground, for the drying winds and driving snow pruned all branches that grew vertically. Buds and berries covered these shrubs in season, and must have attracted enormous numbers of birds and mammals, just as they do today in the Arctic.

The dense ground cover provided excellent nesting habitats for many birds. Snow buntings, horned larks and snowy owls now nest in such thick shrubbery in the Arctic and likely did so here during the Palaeo-Indian period. This was also the time when the Minas Basin was slowly filling with water and flooding the surrounding lowlands, providing an ideal habitat for wading birds and waterfowl.

Ptarmigan are partridge-like birds that now live in the north. They probably lived here during the post-glacial period. Ptarmigan are well adapted to live in such an environment. In winter they are white with black tails but, when on the ground, the wings conceal the tails and the birds are perfectly camouflaged against the snow. The black tails show during flight, and possibly act as markers to help keep the flock together. A dense layer of feathers covers the toes in winter, and provides both an insulation and "snowshoes" for walking on soft snow. To survive extremely low temperatures, ptarmigan burrow into the snow where they

Ptarmigan

find twigs and buds on which to feed, as well as warmth and shelter. In summer, their plumage changes to gray and brown colours, also a good camouflage against the background of rocks and lichens.

Caribou

The archaeological record shows that caribou were plentiful, and that other tundra mammals, including arctic foxes and arctic hares, lived in the local garden during the Palaeo-Indian period. It also shows that, beluga whales and walruses occurred along the coast. The caribou fed on lichens that were especially abundant on the barrens. The Palaeo-Indian people hunted caribou for food and used the thick pelts to make clothing. Caribou herds migrate along known routes, making them easy to locate and hunt. Caribou are animals of both barrens and mature forests, and they lived in this area for about 12,000 years. When forests replaced the barrens they continued to feed on lichens, and especially on the old man's beard lichen and a ground lichen called, appropriately, "caribou moss". However, the intentional burning of the forests that occurred in the late 1700s and 1800s destroyed extensive areas of these lichens and possibly contributed to the decline of the caribou herds. Caribou have not been present in this area since the early 1900s.

Pre-Ceramic Garden

People continued to move into this region, following the animals on which they depended for food. The early record of the Pre-Ceramic people is incomplete. They, like the Palaeo-Indian people, lived along the coast and many of their artefacts were likely lost with repeated sinking and flooding of the shore. Their later record of some 4000 years ago is better known and continues the story of the natural history of The Old Place.

The Pre-Ceramic garden was completely different from the Palaeo-Indian garden. Studies of fossil pollen show that the climate started to warm about 5000 years ago, and a rich garden of deciduous and coniferous trees gradually replaced the cold garden of dwarf shrubs, sedges and lichens.

The Minas Basin at that time was still smaller than it is now, and the water was shallower and warmer (22°C in summer). The tidal amplitude was then only about one metre, as compared to the fifteen-metre tides of today. However, as water levels rose and the land sank, the seas flowed into the adjacent forests, killed the trees and gradually buried them as sediments built up to form the tidal marshes. The present meadow at The Old Place started to form at that time and overlies this early forest, as do the other marshes and dykelands around the Minas Basin. These processes of sedimentation and marsh formation still continue, at a rate of about 36 centimetres per 100 years.

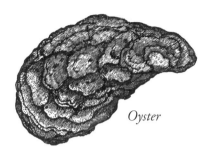

Oyster

Recently, the eroding actions of the tides exposed stumps of this buried forest on a nearby beach, and carbon-dating shows that some of them are 4500 years old. Pine, hemlock and beech were the dominant species, some with trunks measuring a metre in diameter and suggesting trees of about twenty-five metres or more in height. The growth rings are well defined in these fossil trees, and some specimens were 200 years old at the time they were flooded and buried. Birch, elm, oak, poplar, ash and alder were also present, and black spruce and larch grew in poorly drained soils as they do now. Trees of the same species grow here today, but specimens of such size and age are unusual. The ground cover was not preserved, but presumably was the same as that now found under similar tree associations.

Recent erosions also exposed marine shells that are different from those found today. Oysters do not grow now in the Minas Basin, but giant oysters were plentiful in the warmer waters of Pre-Ceramic times. Shells recently exposed measured twenty-five centimetres in length and were carbon-dated to 3800 years ago. Similarly, the early shells of soft-shelled clams were twice the size of present-day clams.

Soft-shelled Clam

The Pre-Ceramic people hunted and fished. White-tailed deer and moose became available as game animals, in addition to caribou, with the growth of the forests. Smaller mammals typical of woodlands, such as red fox, pine martin, black bear and snowshoe rabbit, were present and also hunted for skins and food. As the Minas Basin filled, the water flowed over the surrounding lowlands and created an excellent habitat for geese, ducks and shorebirds

The Pre-Ceramic people also caught swordfish, salmon, gaspereau and sturgeon. Swordfish were apparently a mainstay of their diet for swordfish bones are numerous in refuse piles along the coast. Swordfish prefer warm water, at least 16ºC, and the warmer waters of the Pre-Ceramic period attracted them. When at rest, swordfish circle slowly at the surface and bask in the sun, and such behaviours make them relatively easy to hunt. Pre-Ceramic refuse heaps also contain remains of cod, and gray and harbour seals. To hunt these large animals, the Pre-Ceramic people used harpoons and lances fitted with bone or slate points.

The Pre-Ceramic culture disappeared about 3500 years ago, perhaps again as a consequence of major environmental changes. At that time, the submergence of George's Bank, located off the coast of northern Maine, and the increasing tidal ranges allowed colder water to pour into the Gulf of Maine and Bay of Fundy. As one result, the valued swordfish became scarce, for it presumably moved offshore and farther south into warmer waters. Swordfish remains become less numerous and soft-shelled clams more common in the refuse heaps of the later Pre-Ceramic period.

Small Changes,
Large Effects

Today, we live during a period of climatic warming that is apparently being accelerated by human activity. One sign of change is warm weather earlier in spring and lasting later into autumn. It is difficult to anticipate the effects on our natural history of a temperature change of only a few degrees. To appreciate the possible magnitude of such influences, it is helpful to realize that, globally, the mean annual temperature during the Ice Age was only 5° C colder than it is today, and that the mean annual temperature during the Pre-Ceramic period was only 3° C warmer than today. A change of only a few degrees results in major alterations to plant and animal, including human, populations. While local changes may be more extreme, global changes are the cumulative results of local changes.

MI'KMAQ (MICMAC) GARDENS

The early Mi'kmaq people lived closer to nature than we do. They depended on the plants and animals around them for food and health, and expressed gratitude when they took them for use. Today, many people live apart from the natural world and have lost their appreciation of it. Nevertheless, we are today as dependent on it for food and health as were the early people, and perhaps even more so for recreation, adventure and beauty. Regaining an awareness of the world around us, and an understanding of our impact on it, is the foundation of successful stewardship.

The Mi'kmaq people are part of the Algonquin nation. They lived here as early as 2500 years ago, and their story for the period of about 1000 years ago describes the natural history of the area about The Old Place in the days before the European settlers arrived.

The Mi'kmaq people wintered in the shelter of the forest and hunted moose, beaver and other animals. They summered along the seashores and estuaries where they fished, gathered shellfish, and hunted waterfowl and sea mammals.

The climate was warmer a thousand years ago than it is now. The meadow at The Old Place was a tidal marsh and was bounded to the west by a steep bank. The Mi'kmaq people had a summer camp on this bank. The site was an appropriate one: it was sheltered, there were freshwater springs and streams nearby, it offered a view over the marsh, fish and birds were abundant on the marsh, and the tide quickly carried their canoes to and from the estuary. Today, there are homes and stores on this campsite.

Nebookt is the Mi'kmaq word for "woods". Much of the land in the area of The Old Place is now cleared for agriculture, but when the Mi'kmaq people lived here a mature forest extended down the hill to the marsh. Beautiful stands of red and white pines, hemlock, beech, sugar maple, and yellow and white birches made up this forest, and there were lesser numbers of other species.

The Mi'kmaq people used trees in many ways. Apart from

Nebookt

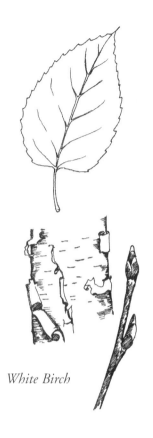

White Birch

White Ash

wood for their fires and tools, they used bark to cover wigwams and canoes and to make containers of various types, roots to make rope and other types of bindings, boughs for bedding, sap and gum for caulking and waterproofing, strips of wood for weaving baskets, and dyes from bark and roots to decorate their clothing and other possessions.

The Mi'kmaq people used the bark of white birch to cover their wigwams. The smaller wigwams were conical in shape and constructed by erecting a frame of poles and covering it with bark, skins and mats woven with reeds. They sewed the sheets of bark together with fine roots, often roots of black spruce which are pliable and resistant to water, and they decorated the bark with scenes of wildlife. When camp was moved, they steamed the bark to make it less brittle, rolled it up and took it to the next site.

They also used birch bark to cover their canoes. The canoes ranged in length from three metres for river use to eight metres for ocean use. Again, they sewed the bark over a wooden frame with split spruce roots, and sealed the seams with spruce gum. The cross-bars and paddles were made of beech, maple or ash and were often elaborately decorated.

White birch trees still grow at The Old Place. The larger ones have trunks that measure almost two metres in circumference — large enough to cover a canoe. The white bark, with papery curls, is distinctive. The winter twigs also aid identification: a zigzag design with pointed buds and usually three catkins. Birch flowers in spring and the seeds mature in autumn. Many songbirds, especially pine siskins and redpolls, search through the twigs for seeds and fragments of catkins. The wind sprinkles the winged seeds over the early snows of December.

The wood of white ash is noted for its toughness, resilience and light weight. The Mi'kmaq people used white ash for tools, snowshoe frames, paddles, weaving and basketry. They made snowshoe frames by soaking the wood and bending it into an oval shape, and then weaving a network of rawhide thongs across the centre, often using thongs cut from the uncured skin of moose. Ash was the preferred wood for basketry. Pounding causes the wood to separate along its annual growth rings, enabling the basket-maker to peel off thin strips. The strips were dyed and woven into baskets.

Today, there are a number of white ash trees at The Old Place. Their identification is easy: the leaves are divided into leaflets, and the winter buds are large, rounded and oppositely arranged. Ash trees are either male or female and flower in spring. However, they produce large clusters of seeds only every second or third year. Each seed is flat and has a single wing. Maple seeds are similar, but are paired and have two wings. Many species of birds and especially waxwings and pine grosbeaks feast on ash seeds. Large clusters of winged seeds occasionally remain on the trees throughout winter. These are the products of flowers infested with gall-mites, and are not attractive to birds.

Shrubs and small trees like mountain maple, striped maple, hazelnut, dogwoods and viburnums formed the understory of local woods in early Mi'kmaq times, as they do now. The Mi'kmaq name for the mountain behind the village is *Owbogegechk*, a word that means "abounding in dogwood". Both red osier and alternate-leaved dogwoods still grow abundantly on the mountain, but were lost from the lower lands as they were cleared for agriculture. However, we transplanted both shrubs to The Old Place. Red osier dogwood grows in thickets and has red stems. Alternate-leaved dogwood grows singly and reaches the height of a small tree. Its twigs are greenish and often streaked with white. The leaves and buds of red osier dogwood are arranged in opposite pairs, unlike those of alternate-leaved dogwood. Both dogwoods provide an abundance of food for birds and mammals.

The early Mi'kmaq people prepared a solution from the bark and roots of both dogwoods and used it to bathe sore eyes. Also, they made "kinnikinnik" from the dried inner bark and leaves of dogwood, as well as from other trees and shrubs. Kinnikinnik, mixed with tobacco, was used for ceremonial smoking and had a soothing effect.

Nebooktook means "in the woods". While records of the herbaceous plants that grew here during early Mi'kmaq times are sketchy, the plant species were likely the same as now and typical of the forest type.

Owbogegechk

Alternate-leaved Dogwood

Nebooktook

Red-stemmed
Feather-moss

Step-moss

Thick layers of needles and moss carpeted the ground in the coniferous forests, making it possible to walk easily and quietly in all directions. Red-stemmed feather-moss and step-moss probably formed much of this ground cover, for today they are common mosses in coniferous woods. Red-stemmed feather-moss, or Schreber's moss, trails over the ground and forms loose mats, but its overlapping leaves partly conceal the red colour of its stems. Step-moss shows a different leaf pattern. The new growth arises in a layered or step-like fashion, and the older plant consists of a series of "steps" with each step representing one year's growth. The leaves are clustered on the steps, giving the plant a fern-like appearance. It is also called mountain-fern moss and is one of our many beautiful mosses.

Wood sorrel was likely common in the Mi'kmaq forest. It grows in openings, often where a tree has fallen and sunlight reaches the floor. Sorrel prefers moist areas and often grows in beds of red-stemmed feather moss. The leaves are dark green and arranged in three leaflets like a shamrock. Its flowers are single and white with red veins, although some flowers are rose-coloured with purplish veins.

Bloodroot and goldthread grew in the woods during early Mi'kmaq times, as they do today. Bloodroot is a member of the poppy family and has large white flowers. The flowers appear in early May while the young leaves are still wrapped around the stems. Once they unfold, the leaves are large and rounded with uniquely scalloped edges. The Mi'kmaq people extracted a red or orange dye from bloodroot and used it to colour skins, and later the European settlers used it to colour wool and flax. They also used bloodroot for medicinal purposes.

Goldthread produces white flowers in late spring and early summer. It grows in moist habitats, often in mossy sites and mixed with wood sorrel. Its leaves are shiny, evergreen and divided into three leaflets. The underground stems are bright yellow, thus its name. Both the Mi'kmaq people and the early settlers prepared a drink by boiling the stems, and used it as a general tonic, to treat stomach disorders and mouth sores, and to bathe sore eyes. The Mi'kmaq people also extracted a yellow dye from goldthread and used it to colour the feathers and porcupine quills that they used

Woodland Flowers

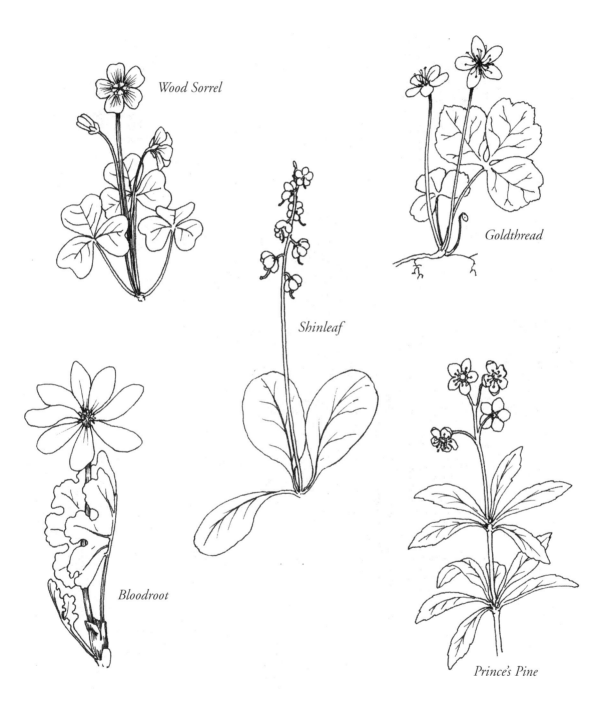

Wood Sorrel

Goldthread

Shinleaf

Bloodroot

Prince's Pine

to decorate their clothing. Both the Mi'kmaq people and early settlers used this dye to colour skins, wool and flax.

Shinleaf and prince's pine flowered in mid summer during Mi'kmaq times, as they do now. These are evergreen plants and grow in openings and along woodland paths. The flowers of shinleaf are white, bell-shaped with a long pistil, and hang from a short stem. Its leaves are clustered at the base of the plant. Prince's pine, as its name suggests, often grows under pine trees. Its flowers are pink and white, highly fragrant, and clustered at the ends of the branches. The shiny leaves are arranged in whorls.

The Mi'kmaq people and the early settlers used both shinleaf and prince's pine for medicinal purposes. Shinleaf is so named because its leaves were used to treat injuries in the same way that a "shin-plaster" was used. They were applied to an injury either as whole leaves or were crushed to make a salve. Prince's pine was used in a similar way, and a tea was also prepared from its leaves for use as a tonic and to treat colds. Both plants promoted healing for, as is now known, they contain antibacterial chemicals, a high content of Vitamin K, and the pain-easing salicylates. Another common name for prince's pine is *pipsissewa*. It is from a Cree word that means "to break into small pieces", and describes the plant's beneficial effect in treating gall stones and kidney stones.

Poquahock

Quahog

The Mi'kmaq people fished and collected shellfish about the Minas Basin in the days when they had a summer camp in the area of The Old Place. Today, we find the same species of shellfish, but they are smaller and less abundant and the once numerous collecting areas are now limited by contamination. The larger size of the shellfish in early Mi'kmaq times may reflect the warmer climate of that period, although today's practice of overharvesting also leads to reduced size.

An examination of local middens shows that the early Mi'kmaq people collected soft-shelled clams, as did the Pre-Ceramic people, as well as mussels, razor clams and bar clams. Quahogs are common in early middens, and present through several strata indicating their use for food over a long time. The name "quahog" comes from *poquahock*, an Algonquin word that means "dark shell", for the colour of the shell varies from white to dark purple. The shells were used for money and decorations, and the darker shells had the greater value. The scientific name for quahog is *Mercenaria* which , like the word "merchandise", refers to this commercial use.

Local Mi'kmaq campsites contain the remains of several species of fish, including: gaspereau, Atlantic salmon, rainbow smelt, Atlantic sturgeon, American eel and American shad. Each spring enormous numbers of anadromous fish enter the Minas Basin and migrate up to the freshwater lakes and tributary streams to spawn. Anadromous fish hatch in fresh water, move to the sea until they mature, and then return to fresh water to spawn. This cycle, however, is one that is easily interrupted by the construction of causeways and hydro dams. Today, in rivers about the Minas Basin, smelt still move upstream in April, gaspereau in May and early June, and salmon make several runs during the summer.

The Mi'kmaq name for the gaspereau is *segoonumak*. Locally, the gaspereau run begins when water temperatures reach 9° or 10° C, and the fish are so numerous that they are easily scooped out with a net. In the lakes, each female sheds over 100,000 eggs and then returns to the sea. Nova Scotian gaspereau spawn for each of several years, unlike more southerly fish that spawn only once and die. The young gaspereau hatch in about six days, but remain in the lakes until autumn and early winter. Then they move downstream to the sea and attract fish-eating birds, including mergansers and eagles, in large numbers. At sea, gaspereau congregate into huge schools that remain along the coast not far from the river mouths, and swarm over the tidal marshes to feed when the tide is high.

In early Mi'kmaq times as now, flounder were caught over the expansive tidal flats and marshes. Flounders are flatfish, a term used to describe several species of fish that lie on their wide, flattened sides. They lie on the bottom, partially buried but with both eyes protruding like short periscopes above the sand. Flounders have the ability to raise and lower their eyes and to turn one independently of the other, and in such ways they are able to greatly extend their fields of vision. Also, flounders can change colours to match the background, a practice that both camouflages them

Segoonumak

Gaspereau

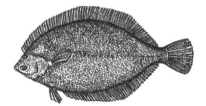

Flounder

from predators and conceals them when hunting. The winter flounder is the flatfish now most frequently caught.

Apcheehkumoochwaakade

The area around The Old Place has long been an excellent one for waterfowl. *Apcheehkumoochwaakade* is the Mi'kmaq name for the uplands on the opposite side of the meadow. It has been variously translated as "a place abounding in little ducks", "home of the black duck" and "duckland". The Mi'kmaq people hunted waterfowl and shorebirds with bows and arrows and with nets and clubs.

In Mi'kmaq times, before the dykes were built, small rafts of common eiders, surf scoters and white-winged scoters (perhaps no black scoters), and large rafts of black ducks foraged over the marsh when the tide was high. In winter, oldsquaw ducks whistled offshore, for their bones are also in local middens of that time. The species seen today along the river are freshwater birds. Black ducks inhabit both salt and fresh water, green-winged teal and blue-winged teal are common, and all three nest along the river and on the meadow. In early Mi'kmaq times, they were also plentiful on freshwater ponds and streams.

Teamook

Specimens from middens show that the early Mi'kmaq people hunted beaver, muskrat, deer, rabbit, river otter and moose. They also hunted the harbour seals that came up the creek to the marsh. Since then, the gradual clearing of land for development, has pushed the beaver back to the forests and streams on the mountains. Otters are now scarce although two appeared on the river one June a few years ago and stayed all summer. We saw them regularly on our morning walks, but they are the only ones that we have seen at The Old Place. Muskrat are still numerous about the river, as are deer and rabbits in adjacent woods. However, the seals and other marine mammals were excluded when the dykes were constructed, although they are still regular visitors to the Basin.

Teamook is the Mi'kmaq word for moose. Moose were plentiful in the early Mi'kmaq garden. While moose provided a primary source of meat, use was made of all parts of the carcass. The skin was used to make clothing, footwear, containers, and

Moose

rawhide thongs for bindings and snowshoes; tools were made from antlers and needles from bones; tendons were pounded to separate the fibres that were then used as sewing threads; and the bladder was used as a container in which to store the oils obtained from marine mammals and birds.

Moose are animals of forested areas, where they forage on aquatic plants along the borders of lakes and swamps and browse on shrubs and trees. After the first settlers dyked the tidal marshes, the moose also browsed on the meadows. Moose increased in numbers in the 1800s. This was a time of cutting and burning of the forests, and the subsequent young growth provided an abundance of browse. They remained numerous into the 1900s and occasionally visited the meadow at The Old Place until about 60 years ago. However, between the 1930s and 1960s, competition from the increasing deer population and "moose sickness" led to the collapse of the local moose population. Moose sickness is caused by a parasitic worm that affects the nervous system and leads to paralysis and death.

It was not unusual to see a moose in the area of The Old Place a few decades ago. We recall visiting an elderly gentleman on the mountain, standing on his doorstep and watching as he lifted his birch-bark horn and, within a few moments, called a moose to the edge of his field. On another occasion, we saw a cow moose and two calves as we canoed down a wooded stillwater. Moose are no longer present in this area, but their recovery in neighbouring regions offers the hope that we may see them here again and, if anyone remembers how, we can try to "call one up".

Nature: Our Past, Present, and Future Needs

Today, we are as dependent on the natural world for food and many of our medicines as were the earlier people. In the immediate future, we will rely to an even greater extent on the diversity of living things for the clues and genetic information needed to produce new medicines, and to develop new food varieties that can produce high yields under changing conditions for growth. Increasingly, people will turn to natural places for relaxation, adventure and beauty. Natural sites must be protected, and those about our communities help fulfill special needs.

ACADIAN GARDEN

The natural history of an area changes continuously. A "nature walk" through history illustrates past changes and helps explain those that continue to occur. It shows what the landscape was once like, and provides the long-term view needed to help distinguish natural changes from those caused by human activities. Can your community re-establish a natural area with plants typical of a particular period in its history?

The French settlers, or Acadians, came to this region in the years following 1680. Many came from the west coast of France where they had built dykes to claim meadows from tidal marshes. This background undoubtedly made the Minas Basin area attractive to them for its expansive tidal marshes could also be dyked and developed into highly fertile fields.

In 1714 there were several Acadian homes only a short distance from the site now occupied by The Old Place, and by 1750 the population had grown to 225 people. Undoubtedly, they travelled and hunted throughout the area, and canoed and fished along the nearby marshes.

Acadian life was closely tied to the natural environment. In summer they farmed, built and repaired dykes, and fished. In winter they cut fire wood and lumber, made clothing from wool and flax, and hunted and trapped. Through the years, they developed prosperous farms and comfortable homes where singing and dancing added cheer to the tasks of developing the land.

Homes Their first homes were of simple construction; but once their farms were established and marshlands dyked, the Acadians built more substantial homes on the uplands overlooking the dyked fields. The first homes contained a single room, a loft, and a small cellar for storing root crops. They built their houses almost entirely from materials that were locally available. Many were built of squared logs, dove-tailed to form the corner joints, and chinked with marsh clay mixed with salt-meadow cordgrass for binding. They used split boards for flooring, slate tiles for the hearth, and field stone and clay for the fireplace and chimney. The fireplace contained an oven.

Doors and window shutters were also made of split wood, fastened together with wooden pegs or hand-wrought nails, and hung with hinges of leather. The roof was thickly thatched with overlapping bundles of salt-marsh cordgrass. In some homes, the interior walls and ceilings were insulated with a thick layer of marsh clay, again mixed with salt-meadow cordgrass for binding, and surfaced with a thin layer of white clay to create a plaster-like finish.

The Acadians planted both vegetable and flower gardens about their homes. In 1740, James Wibault wrote that the marsh soil yielded an "abundance of pulse [legumes], Roots and all kinds of Herbage The winters are long and Severe but nature has made up for the (shortness?) of Summer by giving to all vegetables a quick growth". The Acadians grew vegetables such as rutabaga, beans, lettuce, sage, parsley, rosemary and onions. They imported plants, such as spearmint, sorrel and caraway, for cooking purposes and others, like wormwood, to flavour drinks. The Acadians also grew flax and spun its fine fibres into threads and wove these threads into linen fabric for clothing.

The Acadians planted a variety of imported flowers, many for ornamental purposes. They introduced white campion, or evening lychnis, a member of the pink family. Like other pinks, it has swollen nodes and flowers with five deeply-notched petals. Today, white campion grows with other wildflowers along the edge of the meadow. Its flowers are highly fragrant and open during the evening and at night. White campion attracts nectar-seeking moths and a visit at night with a flashlight is a worthwhile one.

Other "Acadian" flowers still grow on the meadow. Cuckoo-flowers turn areas of the meadow white in May, ragged-robins form patches of pink in June, and bouncing-bets produce white and pink flowers in mid summer. The yellow flowers of silvery cinquefoil carpet the meadow path throughout much of the summer. Its stems and leaves have a white-woolly covering that creates the silvery appearance.

The Acadians also introduced plants for medicinal pur-

Flower Gardens

White Campion

Acadian Flowers

Bouncing-Bet

Ragged-Robin

Cuckoo-flower

Chicory

poses. They made a tea from tansy to drink as a general tonic and to treat colds and fevers, and they extracted an oil from it that, because of its toxic properties, was used to treat parasitic worms. Teas were also made from Joe-pye-weed, mixed with powders of other herbs, for use in the treatment of colds and stomach disorders. Chicory and elecampane were planted for both medicinal and culinary purposes.

The Acadians introduced white and rose-coloured yarrows, and today both grow along the meadow path at The Old Place. They flower in late July and August. Some flowers are white, others are rose, and many are white and turn reddish as they become older. Both colour forms belong to the same species, and the unusual colour combinations result from the two interbreeding. Their scientific name is *Achillea,* after the hero of Greek mythology. The leaves are finely divided and another name for yarrow is milfoil, a word that means a "thousand leaves". The leaves contain a substance that clots blood, and Achilles used the crushed leaves to treat soldiers wounded in battle. The Greek poet Homer also asked (in *Ileid*) to have his wounds treated with Achilles' solution.

Yarrow

The early settlers ground all parts of the yarrow plant into powder, and made a tonic from it for use as a general cure-all. Its effects were beneficial because, as is now known, yarrow contains large amounts of such minerals as iron, calcium and sulphur. The settlers also made various types of teas by mixing yarrow powder with powders of other plants, and used them to treat colds, fevers and other symptoms.

These are only a few of the more than eighty species of plants that were first introduced to this area by the Acadians. The Acadians also established field habitats by dyking the tidal marshes and cutting the forests, practices that continue today. These new habitats encouraged many of the introduced plants to spread widely and they are now among our most common field and roadside species.

Farm animals roamed freely and foraged along the roadsides and through the woods about the villages. The Acadian farmers planted thick hedges around their gardens to protect their

Trees and Shrubs

Buckthorn

crops from both domestic and wild animals. The shrubs used included native and European hawthorns and the imported and fast-growing buckthorns.

Today, buckthorn bushes are numerous on the meadow at The Old Place. They flower in early June, but their yellowish flowers are small and generally inconspicuous. The abundant fruit, on the other hand, is distinctive: shiny black, fleshy and contains two hard seeds. It forms along the twigs by mid August and remains on the shrubs until eaten. Robins, grosbeaks, waxwings, pheasants and starlings feast on the fruit. After gorging themselves, the birds perch in trees and along fences where they digest the fleshy part and eliminate the seeds. We must cut the young buckthorns away from the fences every few years, a good demonstration that birds distribute seeds to all parts of the property and beyond.

The Acadians also planted shrubs and small trees for ornamental purposes and for fruit to make jams and jellies. They imported European cranberry (a viburnum, not a true cranberry), red fly-honeysuckle, choke-cherry and black cherry. Red fly-honeysuckle is still a frequently planted ornamental, but in the wild it has remained largely in areas of Acadian homesteads and is a good marker to assist in finding such sites. Choke-cherry and black cherry have spread widely and are today common shrubs along roads, in old fields and in woodland clearings. Curiously, these kinds of shrubs are the ones that we now plant to attract birds and other wildlife to our properties. Were the Acadians birdwatchers?

Daphne was one of their ornamental shrubs. Cultivated daphne is now often planted, but wild shrubs, descendants of the Acadian plants, still grow in neighbouring woodlands and often not far from sites of the Acadian homes. Several years ago, we rescued a wild plant from an area being cut and it is now growing beside our driveway. Daphne is a small shrub that flowers in late April and is the first woodland shrub to bloom each spring. It flowers before the leaves appear, and the pinkish-purple sprays are a welcome beginning to the colours of spring. The flowers are small, clustered along the stems, and each is formed of four sepals in the form of a cross. The leaves unfold in mid May and the fruit, which is poisonous, turns bright red in September.

In Greek mythology Daphne was a mountain nymph, a

spirit in the form of a beautiful maiden. She was pursued by Apollo and, as he was about to catch her, she called to Mother Earth for help. Mother Earth spirited her to another island and left a flowering shrub in her place. Actually the shrub was a laurel bush, a taxonomic slip perhaps explained by Daphne's haste to escape.

The Acadians also planted shade trees and orchards about their homes. They planted Lombardy poplar for ornamental purposes, wind-breaks, and to mark boundaries and driveways, for it grows rapidly and provides a good shelter. It is planted today for the same purposes. The Acadians also imported French willow for use as a shade tree and to mark boundaries and roads. Today, scattered clumps of this willow still grow in ravines about the Minas Basin, although there are none at The Old Place. Periodically, they are decimated by willow-blight fungus, but new shoots grow from roots that likely trace their origins back to the stock planted by the Acadians. Orchards of Caville, Rambour and Reinette apple trees were planted, as were pear, plum, and sweet and sour cherry trees.

The Acadians hunted moose, occasionally caribou and deer, rabbits, ruffed and spruce grouse, white partridge (ptarmigan), ducks, geese and shorebirds. The climate was colder in Acadian times than it is now, for they lived here during the "Little Ice Age". Snow started in early October and continued into April. Because of the colder climate, some animal species that lived here then are now rare or found only in more northern regions.

Several mammals lived here during Acadian times that are not present now. About 1750 the English government confiscated all guns from the Acadian people. The Acadians listed, among other reasons, the need to protect their domestic animals from wolves in their petition to have their guns returned. Wolves are nomadic animals and small hunting packs were regularly reported here during the latter part of the 1700s. In 1796 the government passed an act "to encourage the killing of wolves". The wolf remained part of the local fauna until the mid 1880s.

Marten were common during Acadian times, and the Mi'kmaq people used marten skins to make ceremonial robes. Through the 1700s and early 1800s, marten were sufficiently

Daphne

Mammals and Birds

Spruce Grouse

Fisher

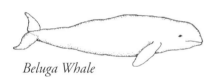

Beluga Whale

numerous that they were hunted and about 1000 pelts exported each year. However, the population dropped during the late 1880s, and now marten are extremely rare and are listed as an endangered species in parts of eastern Canada. Similarly, the fisher, then called the peccan, was hunted during the 1700s and early 1800s and its pelt sold. Their numbers also dropped in the late 1800s and for many decades a sighting was most unusual. Today, however, reintroductions have been successful and local reports of fisher sightings are becoming more frequent.

The Acadians hunted "white porpoises", with some measuring about five metres in length. The blubber of one "porpoise" yielded up to three barrels of oil, "one for home use and two to be sold". White porpoises are beluga whales and were once regular visitors to the Minas Basin and the Bay of Fundy. Today, the main population of belugas in southeastern Canada is in the St. Lawrence River where they are classified as an endangered species. Belugas now visit Nova Scotian waters only occasionally. The colder climate likely explains their presence here during Acadian times, when other northern species, including walrus, also occurred along the Nova Scotian coast.

Shellfish and Fish

Along the shore, the Acadians collected mussels, clams, whelks, and periwinkles. The latter two were known as "Champlain's escargot". The Acadians also supplemented their food supplies with fish. Then as now, enormous numbers of fish entered the Minas Basin and migrated up its tributary rivers to spawn. The migrations began in early spring when smelt and later gaspereau moved up the rivers. Striped bass entered the tidal rivers to spawn in June, and salmon arrived in spring and again in autumn. Also, beginning in late June and continuing through summer, large schools of shad migrated into the Basin to feed and formed the basis of a major fishery.

Marine species such as cod, halibut, pollock and haddock were caught, as were capelin and sturgeon. Today, capelin occur in more northern waters and are not common about Nova Scotia. Sturgeon still occur in the Minas Basin and are joined in June and July by sturgeon that are migrating along the eastern coast of North America. These migrating sturgeon are large, measuring

Sturgeon

two to three metres in length. Sturgeon have a flair for jumping and leap completely clear of the water. They jump most frequently during the time of slack water that occurs just after high tide. A two-metre fish leaping into the air is a spectacular sight!

The English deported the Acadians, beginning in 1755. Families were transported by ship to various locations between New England and Georgia, and their homes and barns were burned. Although they lived here for only 75 years, they brought the art of dyke-building that has since made major changes to local land use, and they introduced many species of plants to the local flora. Today, because of the Acadians, we might discover a daphne shrub in full blossom while exploring among the "murmuring pines and hemlocks".

Deportation

Fields in this area are the product of human activity and many field plants are introduced species. Some of the early plants are now scarce and difficult to find. Also, here as elsewhere, present areas of old-growth woodlands are small and scattered. Can your community establish a "historic field" or allow a woodlot to progress to an "old" forest? Such sites preserve the natural history of our communities, and tell us about the earlier people who lived closer to the natural world than we do. "Historic Gardens" are full of information, they are living museums. A nature walk through history can be highly informative.

A Nature Walk Through History

1800S GARDEN

In the area of The Old Place, as elsewhere, people have dramatically altered the landscape while earning their livelihood. Nevertheless, we are still able to explore a variety of habitats and enjoy the remarkable diversity of plants and animals that live in them. Present-day communities and individuals must accept the responsibility of conserving this diversity of living things, so that future generations may continue to know the pleasures and challenges that the natural world has given us.

The early farmers cleared much of the land between the dyked meadows and the mountain during the late 1700s and early 1800s. In clearing their woodlands, usually during winter, they cut the trees about a metre above ground, let them dry until summer and then burned them. Often the farmers sowed the land with rye, harrowing it in between the stumps, or planted potatoes for a few years until the stumps rotted and could be pulled out with a yoke of oxen. Alternatively, they pastured cattle in the cleared woods until the stumps were removed. Workers received about twenty shillings a day for cutting and burning the woods.

Trees
        The Old Place was built in the mid 1800s. The tree species in the woodlands at that time were the same as those present today, but deciduous trees were more numerous. Species like red maple, sugar maple, yellow birch and beech grew on the mountain; while red spruce, eastern hemlock and white pine filled the ravines and covered the lower slopes. These were giant trees of a mature forest that had never been cut. Today, with successive cuttings and regrowths, most trees are smaller and evergreens predominate. Large areas of white spruce, balsam fir and poplar now grow on the mountain, species typical of the early stages of forest succession.

        A stand of beech trees is an attractive place to visit. The bark is smooth and bluish-gray, and the trees often grow in clusters from shoots rising from the roots. The leaves are large and elliptical, dark green in summer and leathery and bronze in winter. Many leaves remain on the trees in winter, especially on younger growth, and rustle gently in the breezes. The winter buds are shiny and brown and distinctively long and pointed. Every two or three years beech trees produce a good crop of nuts. The nuts grow in prickly husks that split with the first frosts of autumn. They are edible, but hard to find as they are quickly eaten by squirrels, deer, grouse and other wildlife.

When The Old Place was new, beech trees reached a height of twenty-five metres and measured up to a metre in diameter. Today, there are still large stands of beech, but most trees are small and show extensive areas of abnormal growth called cankers. The cankers may kill a tree or so weaken its branches that they break easily during storms. A fungus aided by an insect causes the canker. Beech scale insects pierce the bark to obtain sap and later the beech fungus enters through these injuries. Both insect and fungus came to North America from Europe, the insect in 1890 and the fungus in the 1920s, and continue to spread through our beech woods.

The American chestnut was a common cultivated tree about homes and gardens in the 1800s, but was not a forest tree in this area. The chestnut is a tall, straight tree, up to twenty metres high, with a wide, rounded crown. Its leaves are long and yellowish green, and its creamy white flowers are highly scented. The nuts develop in large burrs that ripen in autumn. They are sweet and edible, and eagerly sought by both people and wildlife. Regrettably, blight attacked the American chestnut beginning about 1900 and destroyed it within a few decades. Today, hopeful that the blight has died out, gardeners are again planting an occasional American chestnut about their homes.

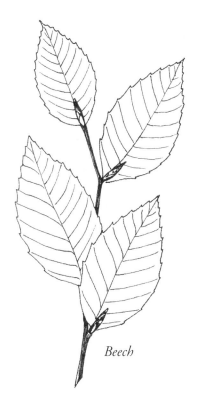

Beech

Some plants that grew in the gardens of the late 1800s are rare today, but others escaped from cultivation and now form a conspicuous part of our floral heritage. Herb gardens were common, peonies were popular as were several early varieties of lilies, and hops were grown to make beer. Some early plants have persisted near the woodland path,

Garden heliotrope or garden valerian, motherwort and common fumitory were once popular plants. Today, they occur in

Cultivated and Naturalized Gardens

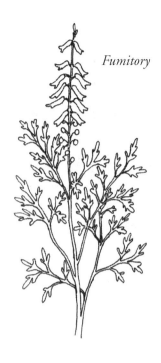

Fumitory

Columbine

this area only rarely, often near old homesteads. Garden heliotrope reaches a metre in height and blooms from mid July through August. Its small flowers are pink and white, funnel-shaped and arranged in small clusters. Motherwort is another tall plant that is now difficult to find. However, the arrangement of flowers in tight whorls about its leaf-stems is a good identification aid. The lilac or pink blossoms are present from June to August. Common fumitory was introduced as a garden flower and was also brought here in ship ballast. It is a climbing plant, reaching a metre in length, and flowers in July and August. The flowers are pink with reddish tips and clustered on a long stalk. The gray-green leaves give the plant a "smoky" appearance, thus its name. Fumitory is also called earth smoke. In early England, people burned fumitory to drive away witches and evil spirits.

Sweet rocket (or dame's rocket), bouncing-bet and columbine were common plants in gardens of the mid 1800s and have since spread widely about The Old Place. Sweet rocket now carpets large areas of the meadow and river bank, and clusters of bouncing bet grow among the field roses on the meadow. Both provide attractive displays of pink and white flowers: sweet rocket in mid June and early July, and bouncing bet in late July and August. Columbine is another escapee that we especially appreciate. It now grows along the garden and woodland paths and blooms in late May and early June. Many flowers are deep red, the wild colour, often with yellow inside, but the blue and white colours of the garden varieties are also present. The flowers are bell-shaped, hanging, and each of the five sepals extends upwards like a spur. The name columbine comes from a Latin word that means "dove-like". According to one explanation, the petals and spurs of the flower resemble five doves drinking from a bowl. The swollen spurs contain the nectar and bees must make a hole in them to reach it. Columbine, especially the red one, is a favourite of hummingbirds.

Several varieties of moss roses and tea roses , including cinnamon rose, grew in the gardens of the mid 1800s. It still grows about old homes and farms in this area, and often forms large thickets because it spreads from shoots rising from the roots. Pink flowers blanket the thickets in early summer. It is called cinnamon rose because the earlier varieties, more so than the newer ones, had a cinnamon fragrance. At one time, the hips were valued in cooking because, like many roses, they contain a high content of vitamin C.

Fishing was an important industry in the 1800s, and shad fishing was a major part of it. In the late 1700s, the shad was described as "the best poor-man's fish of any, for they are so fat of themselves, that they need nothing to make them ready for eating".

It is now known that shad make extended, long-distant migrations. They prefer water temperatures of 12° to 15° C and each summer as the temperature warms, shad from rivers along the eastern coast of North America, many from as far south as Florida, follow the coastal currents north. They enter the Bay of Fundy, circle the Bay and the Minas Basin, and then move south again.

The Mi'kmaq people fished shad and other species, and they used fish traps and weirs. At low tide, they constructed a high fence on the tidal flats that led into a large circular trap. At high tide, the fish followed the fence into the trap, and during the next low tide people walked out over the sandflats to collect them. The Mi'kmaq people taught weir-fishing techniques to the Europeans and weirs continued in use through the 1800s and into the 1900s. Unfortunately, weirs capture everything indiscriminately, including sea turtles and porpoises.

In the 1800s, the people also fished with gill nets and boats equipped with seines. Seine fishing caught enormous numbers of fish. There are local reports of 10,000 shad being caught per tide. These shad were transferred from the fishing boats to scows and hauled up the river to a site just downstream from The Old Place. There they were split and placed on racks on the bank to dry.

The supply of shad appeared to be inexhaustible in the 1800s. However, in the early 1900s the shad disappeared and the fishery collapsed. The reasons were not known at the time. We know now that dam construction and pollution of many of the southern rivers prevented the shad from moving up these streams

Fish

Weir

Shad

to spawn. In recent years, these communities have reduced river pollution and restored the spawning grounds, and the shad population is recovering. Today shad again migrate north in good numbers each summer to circle the Bay of Fundy and the Minas Basin, as they have done for centuries past. The shad story shows that habitat damage is rarely limited to a local effect. It is a good example of how actions taken in one area may influence the fauna of communities located many hundreds of kilometres away. It also illustrates that distant communities can cooperate in conservation programmes and share an economically vital species.

Birds

Birding The Old Place in the mid 1800s, when it was new, produced a species list quite different from the ones we compile today. There are changes both in species present and in many of the names used.

There were small flocks of noisy passenger pigeons about The "New" Place, feeding in the oak and apple trees as did the much larger flocks of fifty years previously. Robins, golden-winged woodpeckers (now called flickers), white-bellied martins (tree swallows) and summer warblers (yellow warblers) were common then as now. Song sparrows were also common, but savannah sparrows, unlike today, were rare. Chewinks, with black and rufous markings, lived in the shrubbery, but today towhees are rare visitors. Flocks of blossom birds (cedar waxwings) arrived in June when the apple trees came into bloom and remained through the summer. Today, they nest at The Old Place, and occasionally stay through winter.

Black-throated Green Warbler

Woodland warblers were also present about The New Place, some with different names from those used today. Magnolia, red-pole (palm), evergreen (black-throated green) and chestnut-sided warblers were regularly seen about woodland openings, but considerable searching was necessary to find the strikingly-coloured hemlock (blackburnian) warbler.

Bronzed (common) grackles and red-winged blackbirds, although numerous today, were either rare or absent about The New Place. Evening grosbeaks were absent, although they now visit throughout the year and nest nearby. It was unusual to see a rose-breasted grosbeak about The New Place, but today we listen to their singing each spring. It was also unusual to see Wilson's (veery) and olive-backed (Swainson's) thrushes, two birds whose songs we now enjoy on spring evenings.

Bob Lincolns sang continuously and nested on the meadows each spring. Bobolinks are still present, but are decreasing in numbers. There were a few marsh snipe (pectoral sandpipers) along the river and they still stop during migration. Ortolans (soras) were regularly seen in the reeds and likely nested here, but it requires lots of good luck to find one today.

Barred and great horned owls were common about The New Place, and hawk-owls occurred from time to time during winter although their numbers were then declining. Barred and great horned owls still live on the mountain and in the evening glide down to hunt over the meadow and along the river. Hawk-owls are no longer present.

Goshawk

The common hawk about The New Place was the goshawk. They are still present on the mountain, although fewer in number, and most years we find a nest. Actually, it is difficult not to find their nesting site for they start screaming and diving at us when we walk within fifty metres of it. Today, the red-tailed hawk is the common one, although red-tailed buzzards were rare about The New Place. Marsh hawks (harriers) sailed over the dykelands 150 years ago as they do today, but it was unusual then to see rough-legged hawks although they are now regular visitors in winter.

House sparrows were introduced in 1878, a decade after The Old Place was built, and today are part of the local avifauna. Two local farmers and orchardists introduced them, releasing them on the uplands along the opposite side of the Habitant River. The birds, obtained in New England, were presumably descendants of the ones released two decades earlier in New York. In introducing them here, the hope was that the birds would proliferate and help control insects that were damaging crops. They did proliferate and soon became an "abundant" resident, but they deserted the crop lands and took up residence about towns and farm buildings.

Mammals

Mammals were numerous in local woodlands during the late 1700s and early 1800s. Mouse-deer (moose) occurred "in great plenty", with some weighing 80 stone, and "carraboes", bear, beaver, porcupine and wildcat were abundant. Also present were otter, mink, sable (weasel), marten, fisher, musquash (muskrat), red squirrel and flying squirrel. Today, there are no moose, caribou, or marten in the area about The Old Place, but the other species can still be found, some on a regular basis and others only occasionally.

Deer were not numerous during much of the 1800s. They were present in early Mi'kmaq times, but later, during the 13th and 14th centuries, the climate became colder and this "Little Ice Age" continued into the early 1800s. The deeper snows apparently contributed to a decline in the deer population, and deer were scarce when the Europeans were establishing their settlements. However, the cutting of forests and abandonment of farms in the later 1800s and early 1900s provided the ideal deer habitat of open woods and young growth and, together with new immigrations and introductions, viable breeding populations were re-established.

Deer

Today, we see deer tracks everywhere when we are skiing on the mountain. On a ski trip a few years ago, we found a deer yard in an old deserted orchard. Tracks, signs of browsing, and prints where the deer had bedded down suggested that thirty deer yarded there. Today, on spring evenings, deer come out of the woods to graze on the fields, and occasionally one or two come down to the meadow at The Old Place.

Special Effort Needed

Many changes have occurred in plant and animal populations during the past 150 years. Some species are no longer present, many have decreased in number and some are more plentiful. Change continues, but now at an accelerating rate because human activity increasingly alters the required summer and winter habitats. A special effort is needed to conserve wildlife habitats about our communities, so that future generations may continue to enjoy the diversity of living things that we take for granted.

NATURE'S GARDEN

" 'Mid task and toil, a space
To dream on Nature's face!"

Birch and Paddle
Charles G.D. Roberts (1886)

COMMUNITY GARDENS

Natural sites that are readily accessible to people must be a part of every community's plan for development, and local naturalists must encourage others to visit these sites and help them gain an understanding and appreciation of nature. In such ways, a greater number of people will come to know a piece of the natural world and will accept the responsibility of looking after it.

An Elm Tree and a Community

A few years ago, we watched as workers cut down an elm tree at The Old Place. It had died of Dutch elm disease and had to be removed before other trees became infected. The tree was almost four metres in circumference and more than 300 years old. There were no dykes or aboiteaux when this tree started to grow and the tide flowed to the foot of the wooded hill twice each day. This elm grew beside a stream, now diverted, that once flowed down the hill and out onto the tidal marsh.

The Mi'kmaq people had a summer camp on the nearby upland when this tree was a seedling, from which they could launch their canoes and be carried to and from the Basin by the tide. They likely had a path that passed beside this tree for they surely would have hunted along the shore. This tree was almost ten metres tall when the French settlers arrived and started dyking and draining the tidal marshes. The French established a settlement down river and another on the upland across the creek, and likely travelled along the path with their ox-drawn carts carrying produce and supplies between the communities. When the English became established, they widened this path into a road along which they could drive their horse-drawn carriages. Still later, this road became "Main Street", lined with tall trees on both sides and along which an ongoing stream of cars and trucks now pass.

When this elm tree was young, the climate was colder than it is now; the snow was deeper and remained for a longer time.

Elm

Unlike today, there were caribou and moose here, and packs of wolves hunted along the shore. This tree grew at the edge of a forest, for the land then had not been cleared for agriculture. Giant hemlock, pine, beech, sugar maple and yellow birch grew here, and there were lesser numbers of white ash, red oak and other species.

This elm witnessed the growth of the early community into a bustling town, with a busy harbour and ship building industries, and watched its decline after the era of wooden ships to the status of a small village. The rings of this elm recorded the entire history of the community.

Tremendous changes occurred during the three centuries that this elm stood here, and especially so during the past 50 years. Some changes evolved naturally. They occurred gradually and allowed wildlife time to adjust. Most changes resulted from human activity. They occurred quickly, often unpredictably, and caused significant loss of natural habitats and the plants and animals that lived in them. What will it be like 300 years from now? What will it be like 50 years from now? The last question is the easier one, for it is ours to answer. Can we keep natural places for exploration and beauty about our communities? Will enough people try?

Present attitudes and values must change and many more people must become involved, if we are to conserve the habitats needed to support the diversity of life that we know. If people are to become more receptive to nature they must have access to natural places. There are government programmes for Wilderness Parks, Endangered Spaces and Special Places. While conservation of such sites is essential, they are often remote and access limited. Communities must also provide natural areas, places that can be visited regularly through the seasons and years.

Community places are needed where people can hear the sough of the wind in the pines and listen to the carolling of the thrushes, where they can watch a spider weaving a web or a parula warbler weaving a nest, where they can discover orchids and trilliums, or hunt for seashells and quietly watch shorebirds chasing the waves back and forth. These are places of discovery and places

Community Gardens

White Trilluim

of solace. They are essential if an appreciation of the natural world is to be encouraged.

Natural places were more readily available when I was in school than they are today. I was extremely fortunate to have grown up in a small community that was surrounded by a variety of natural sites. There were estuaries and tidal marshes, varied forest communities, lakes and wetlands, and many of these places attracted significant invasions of migrating fish and birds. Afternoon walks, week-end hikes, and summer camping and canoe trips introduced me to the wonders and excitements of nature. There were always places to explore and "new" plants and animals to discover.

Community
Nature Trusts

Programmes to conserve and restore natural areas are best developed by local government and individuals working together to form "community nature trusts". Ideally, local people should plan community natural sites for they know the areas of special interest and can provide the long-term dedication and leadership needed to care for them. If this is to happen, experienced naturalists must be active in local leadership. Their expertise and perspective must be a part of community planning. Do you have a nature conservation plan for your community? Is it based on careful observation, science and historical information? Preparing such a plan quickly attracts volunteer help and encourages a positive attitude towards the environment.

Gardeners
Needed

Experienced naturalists must also help introduce others to the world of nature. Natural habitats within communities will be conserved only when enough people appreciate and value the plants and animals that live in them. Young people, in particular, must gain an environmental vision if they are to become the community leaders that are needed. Introducing others to nature is now a naturalist's first responsibility.

I grew up in a community that produced many naturalists. Some, now in a variety of professions, continue to enjoy natural history as a hobby. Others became professional biologists, geologists and astronomers. Why has such a small community produced so many naturalists? The answer is a simple one, and one that could apply to all communities: natural sites to explore and naturalists to help.

One autumn when I was in elementary school, I found a group of birds that I could not identify. I described them to a well-known naturalist and asked if he could help me. I now have no doubt that he knew immediately what they were, but he did not tell me. Rather, we talked about them for a while and he suggested I find them again and prepare a written description of them. I followed those birds through the woods for much of the next afternoon and that evening took him a two-page description. Again, I am certain that he recognized them, but he did not say so. Instead, we discussed my notes, I explained some points and he suggested others that I might observe. He was especially interested in the birds' behaviour: were they in shrubs or tree tops and what were they eating? Finally, he noted two characteristics in my description, opened a field guide and helped me identify the birds. They are still one of my favourite species.

There were several respected naturalists in that community and they took a special interest in what my friends and I were doing. They always asked what we had seen, discussed our observations with us and shared their experiences. They suggested places to visit and what to look for, and they loaned us books. My friends and I visited one or more of those naturalists most weeks during all the years that we were in school. They took the time needed to encourage others, and especially to talk to young people.

Encouraging Others: Our First Responsibility

WILDERNESS GARDEN

A diversity of living things is a community treasure. We can keep natural places about our communities, but only if enough people work to protect them. Knowing about them is the first step toward their conservation. We start by becoming familiar with the plants and animals in a special place, and then extending that knowledge to our community and the wilderness beyond.

Cotton-Grass

Dictionaries describe a garden as "an area of land used for the cultivation of flowers, vegetables and trees" ; and also as "a tract of country", "a beautiful region" and "a delightful spot". An undisturbed wilderness is the ultimate garden.

I grew up in a community that is not far from a chain of lakes located on top of a forested upland. When I was in school and early university, a friend and I canoed and camped along those lakes each summer. We explored the woods and streams, and climbed to the tops of the surrounding hills. We sometimes camped on an island near the upper end of the lakes. A family of otters lived nearby and each morning before breakfast, we canoed around the island to watch them sliding down the bank and frolicking in the water. One evening, we canoed down a side-stream to a large meadow and watched a cow moose and two calves feeding along the shore. Each trip lasted for a week or ten days and we compiled lengthy notes about the plants and animals that we found.

Today, I visit those lakes whenever I can. There is a huge granite boulder near shore midway up the lakes that is one of my "special places". It is a pleasant place to sit and watch the wildlife. A pair of common mergansers nests in a tree across the channel, and a pair of black-backed woodpeckers nests in an old weathered stump that stands in the lake about ten metres from shore. It is easy to find the woodpecker nest because the young are so noisy. Cotton-grass grows on the opposite shore and swamp sparrows flit among its stalks.

I try to reach this boulder early in the morning as the sun

is rising and clouds of mist are rolling up off the water. It is then that I can listen to the Swainson's thrushes singing in the woods behind me, and hear the white-throated sparrows declaring the day to be officially under way. Later, after the sun is warmer and the mist has lifted, an adult eagle with its brilliant white head and tail sails down the lake, just above the trees. It returns a short time later and its first patrol of the day is completed. Its nest is in a tall white pine a little farther up the lake.

I drove up to the lakes one February evening a few years ago. There is a woodland trail there that I sometimes hike along in summer. It was a mild evening, the snow was soft, and I put on my skis and started down the path. The ski through the colonnade of trees was a leisurely one. The moon was full and bright, the path glistened, silhouettes of the white pines stood well above the other trees, and clouds of snowflakes blew from the trees and sparkled in the moonlight. I heard a few squeaks, perhaps chickadees or kinglets, a couple of loud chirps, maybe blue jays, and a barred owl that hooted only once from the other side of the lake.

Loon

I stopped to rest on a log beside the frozen lake, and thought of the evening the previous summer when I had come there just to sit and listen to the hermit thrushes carol their even-song and to wait for the calling of the loons. The first call came at dusk, a lingering and lonely note, and was followed hesitatingly by a laughter that gradually rose into a full tremolo; and then the loons started yodelling to the sky, and were joined by the rollicking wails of others further up the lakes until their calls echoed from the hills and through the woods.

Many times I have canoed and camped along that chain of lakes and listened to the loons. We can keep natural places about our communities for exploration and beauty, if enough people understand and treasure them.

> "Where your treasure is, there your heart will be also."
> (Matthew 6: 21)

ACKNOWLEDGEMENTS AND SELECTED REFERENCES

Sherman Boates, Donna Doucet, David Kristie, Richard Stern and Jim Wolford generously took time to read parts or all of the manuscript and offered many helpful suggestions. Their interest and assistance are appreciated. The author originally wrote some species accounts for a weekly *Nature Notes* series published in the *Kentville Advertiser,* and thanks the *Advertiser* for permitting use of this material again in *The Old Place*. Wombat Press of Wolfville, N.S. is also acknowledged for permission to quote from *The Collected Poems of Sir Charles G.D. Roberts*, Desmond Pacey and Graham Adams, Editors, 1985.

     The Old Place is based on many years of watching and reading about nature. Of many excellent books, the following were selected because they were frequently consulted while writing this manuscript. They are listed as a means of acknowledging their use, and also to recommend them for your use should you wish additional reading and information.

Banfield, A.W.F. 1974. *The Mammals of Canada*. National Museums of Canada. Ottawa, Ontario.

Barnes, R.D. 1980. *Invertebrate Zoology*. Saunders College and Holt, Rinehart and Winston. Philadelphia.

Berrill, M. and D. Berrill 1981. *The North Atlantic Coast*. Sierra Club Books. San Francisco.

Carson, Rachel. 1956. *The Sense of Wonder*. Harper & Row. New York and Evanston.

Dana, W.S. 1963. *How To Know The Wild Flowers*. Dover Publications, Inc. New York.

Donly, J.F. 1960. *Identification of Nova Scotia Woody Plants in Winter*. Bull.19. Nova Scotia Dept. of Lands and Forests.

Eiserer, L. 1976. *The American Robin*. Nelson-Hall. Chicago.

Erichsen-Brown, C. 1979. *Medicinal and Other Uses of North American Plants*. Dover Publications, Inc. New York.

Gilhen, J. 1974. *The Fishes of Nova Scotia's Lakes and Streams*. The Nova Scotia Museum. Halifax, Nova Scotia.

Gilpin, J.B. 1882. Shore Birds of Nova Scotia. Proc. Trans. Nova Scotian Inst. Sci. 5: 376-387.

Godin, A.J. 1977. *Wild Mammals of New England*. The John Hopkins University Press. Baltimore and London.

Godfrey, W. Earl. 1966. *The Birds of Canada*. National Museums of Canada. Ottawa, Ontario.

Gotch, A.F. 1981. *Birds - Their Latin Names Explained.* Blandford Press. Poole and Dorset.

Griffin, D., W.Barrett and A. MacKay. 1984. *Atlantic Wildflowers.* Oxford University Press. Toronto

Harrison, H.H. 1984. *Wood Warblers' World.* Simon and Schuster. New York.

Jaeger, E.C. 1978. *A Source-Book of Biological Names and Terms.* 3rd. Ed. Charles C. Thomas, Springfield, Illinois.

Johnsgard, P.A. 1983. *The Hummingbirds of North America.* Smithsonian Institution Press. Washington.

Katona, S.K., V. Rough and D.T. Richardson. 1983. *A Field Guide to the Whales, Porpoises and Seals of the Gulf of Maine and Eastern Canada.* 3rd. Ed. Charles Schibner's Sons. New York.

Leim, A.H. and W. B. Scott 1966. *Fisheres of the Atlantic Coast of Canada.* Fisheries Research Board of Canada.

Martin, J.W. 1977. *The Amphibians and Reptiles of Nova Scotia.* The Nova Scotia Museum. Halifax, Nova Scotia.

McMahar, M.J. and R. Gaugler. 1993. Spatial distribution of hovering male *Tabanus nigrovittatus* (Diptera: Tabanidae). Environ. Entomol. *22*(4): 796-801.

Nero, R.W. 1984. *Redwings.* Smithsonian Institution Press. Washington.

Pasquier, R. 1980. *Watching Birds.* Houghton Mifflin Co. Boston.

Rand, Silas T. 1888. *Dictionary of the Language of the Micmac Indians Who Reside in Nova Scotia, New Brunswick*, etc. Nova Scotia Printing, Halifax, N.S.

Roland A.E. 1982. Geological Background and Physiography of Nova Scotia. The Nova Scotia Institute of Science, Nova Scotia Museum. Halifax, N.S.

Roland, A.E. and E.C. Smith. 1969. *The Flora of Nova Scotia.* The Nova Scotia Museum. Halifax, N.S.

Saunders, G.L. 1970. *Trees of Nova Scotia.* Nova Scotia Dept. of Lands and Forests.

Scott, S.L. (Ed.) 1983. *Field Guide to the Birds of North America.* National Geographic Society. Washington.

Scott, W.B. and E. J. Crossman. 1973. *Freshwater Fishes of Canada.* Fisheries Research Board of Canada, Bull. 184. The Queen's Printer. Ottawa, Ontario.

Stokes, D.W. *A Guide to Nature in Winter* (1976) and *A Guide to the Behaviour of Common Birds* (1979). Little, Brown Co. Boston, Toronto.

Stokes, D.W. and L.Q. Stokes. *A Guide to Bird Behaviour*, Vols. II (1983) & III (1989); and *A Guide to Enjoying Wildflowers* (1985). Little, Brown Co. Boston, Toronto.

Teal, J. & M. 1969. *Life and Death of a Salt Marsh.* Little, Brown Co. Boston, Toronto.

Terres, J.K. 1977. *Songbirds in Your Garden.* Hawthorn Books. New York.

Thurston, H. 1990. *Tidal Life: A Natural History of the Bay of Fundy.* Camden House Publishing. Camden East. Ontario.

Tufts, R.W. 1986. *Birds of Nova Scotia.* 3rd. Ed. Nimbus Publishing Ltd. and The Nova Scotia Museum. Halifax, Nova Scotia.

Wetmore, A. *Song and Garden Birds of North America* (1964) and *Water, Prey, and Game Birds of North America* (1965). National Geographic Society, Washington.

Welty, J.C. 1982. *The Life of Birds.* 3rd Ed. Saunders College Publishing, Philadelphia and New York.

Also recommended:

The Peterson Field Guide Series. Houghton Mifflin Co. Boston.

The Golden Guides to Field Identification. Golden Press. New York.

The Audubon Field Guide Series. Alfred A. Knoff, New York.

ANIMAL AND PLANT INDEX

MAMMALS

BIRDS

AMPHIBIANS and REPTILES

FISH and SHARKS

INVERTEBRATES

TREES and SHRUBS

HERBACEOUS PLANTS

ACTINOMYCETES, BACTERIA, CLUBMOSSES
FERNS, FUNGI, LICHENS and MOSSES